P9-CCR-821

On April 4, 1968, Dr. Martin Luther King, Jr., was assassinated while standing on the balcony outside his room at the Lorraine Motel in Memphis, Tennessee. This is the story of how that motel became the National Civil Rights Museum.

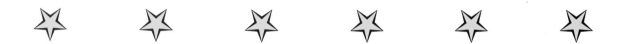

THE NATIONAL CIVIL RIGHTS MUSEUM

CELEBRATES

Everyday People

BY ALICE FAYE DUNCAN

PHOTOGRAPHS BY J. GERARD SMITH

In memory of Sister Thea Bowman—
A. F. D.

To Anne, for all her love and encouragement,
and
for all who dare to dream
I dedicate this book—
J.G.S.

Published by BridgeWater Books, an imprint of Troll Associates, Inc.

Printed in the United States of America.

10 9 8 7 6 5 4 3 2

Library of Congress Cataloging-in-Publication Data

Duncan, Alice Faye.
The National Civil Rights Museum celebrates everyday people / Alice Faye Duncan; photos by J. Gerard Smith.
p. cm.
ISBN 0-8167-3502-6
1. National Civil Rights Museum—Juvenile literature. 2. Afro-Americans—Civil rights—Juvenile literature. 3. Civil rights movements—United States—History—20th century—Juvenile literature. 4. United States—Race relations—Juvenile literature.
I. Smith, J. Gerard. II. Title.
E185.615.D83 1995 326.1'196073'007476819—dc20 94-15831

FOREWORD

The National Civil Rights Museum Celebrates EVERYDAY PEOPLE explores the civil rights movement in America from 1954 to 1968, using select exhibits at the museum as a framework. The lives of some activists have been well documented here, while others may have been left unnoted. Limited space makes it impossible to address the contributions of everyone.

Nevertheless, this book is a tribute to the named and unnamed heroes and heroines who fought for equal rights in the United States of America. It is intended to remind us, page after page, that struggle precedes peace.

Top left and bottom: **The entrance to the Lorraine Motel, now the National Civil Rights Museum.** ***Top right:*** **Michael Pavlovsky's *Movement to Overcome,* a statue in the entrance hall.**

INTRODUCTION

In the city of Memphis, Tennessee, there is a most important motel. It stands downtown at the corner of Calhoun and Mulberry Streets, and everyone who comes through its doors is a welcome guest. Visitors, however, do not check into the motel with luggage, and they never stay overnight. The Lorraine Motel no longer serves as a lodging for weary travelers. Today it is a historic landmark. It is the unforgettable place where America's great dreamer and civil rights leader Dr. Martin Luther King, Jr., was murdered in the spring of 1968.

Even before the death of Dr. King, the motel at 450 Mulberry Street had an interesting history. Originally it was the Windsor Hotel when Walter and Loree Bailey purchased the L-shaped building in 1942. They renamed their new business the Lorraine. For over twenty years, it was one of only a few motels in Memphis where black Americans could get a room for the night. Some of the motel's celebrated clients included such entertainers as Aretha Franklin, B. B. King, and Nat King Cole, as well as baseball legend Jackie Robinson.

Often when Dr. King stopped in Memphis, he stayed at the Lorraine. During these visits, he preached strongly against the mistreatment of black Americans and other people of color. He spoke out against all forms of hatred and encouraged his listeners to protest, march, and boycott to win their rights. He encouraged them to ignore skin color and love all people.

Although the civil rights leader condemned violence and hatred, there were women and men who wanted Dr. King destroyed. They did not want him encouraging people to march and protest until all Americans were given full rights as citizens. They wanted the dreamer killed. And on April 4, 1968, it happened. Dr. King was shot on the second-floor balcony of the Lorraine Motel in Memphis.

Following the tragedy, the Lorraine Motel became a symbol of the civil rights struggle in the United States. Travelers from around the world would come to take pictures of the balcony where Dr. King was killed. Visitors would ask employees questions about that sad day in April. Then they would take home their snapshots and collected stories to share what they had seen.

The next years passed quickly as Dr. King's dream began to come true. Black Americans started to have better job opportunities. Black and white children found themselves going to schools of the same quality, playing at the same parks, and living in the same neighborhoods. Black people could exercise their right to vote, and life in America grew better. But for the Lorraine Motel, times grew worse as criminals, such as drug dealers, moved into the building. Dr. King's death place had become an eyesore—dirty, unkempt, and unsafe.

The balcony of the Lorraine Motel where Dr. King was killed.

Movement to Overcome **inspires visitors by depicting courage and determination.**

Many wondered what would happen to the Lorraine and asked themselves whether it should be saved. For Dr. King's widow, Coretta Scott King, the Lorraine was only a reminder of pain and heartache. She wanted the building torn down. But a group of businesspeople and lawyers in Memphis had a vision. They wanted to turn the old motel into a museum that would capture the sights, sounds, and tensions of the civil rights struggle. They wanted to make the motel a tribute to the common folk, the everyday people, who sang, marched, sat in, boycotted, and went to jail until all Americans were given equal rights under the law. This group called itself the Lorraine Foundation. And in 1982, the members bought the run-down motel in order to make their vision come alive.

Getting state funds and contributions from local businesses to pay for the museum project took a great deal of effort. But the foundation did not give up on its vision and searched until support was found. For three years, the motel remained closed while planning and renovations took place. Then, on August 31, 1991, the great moment arrived. The Lorraine was opened as the country's National Civil Rights Museum.

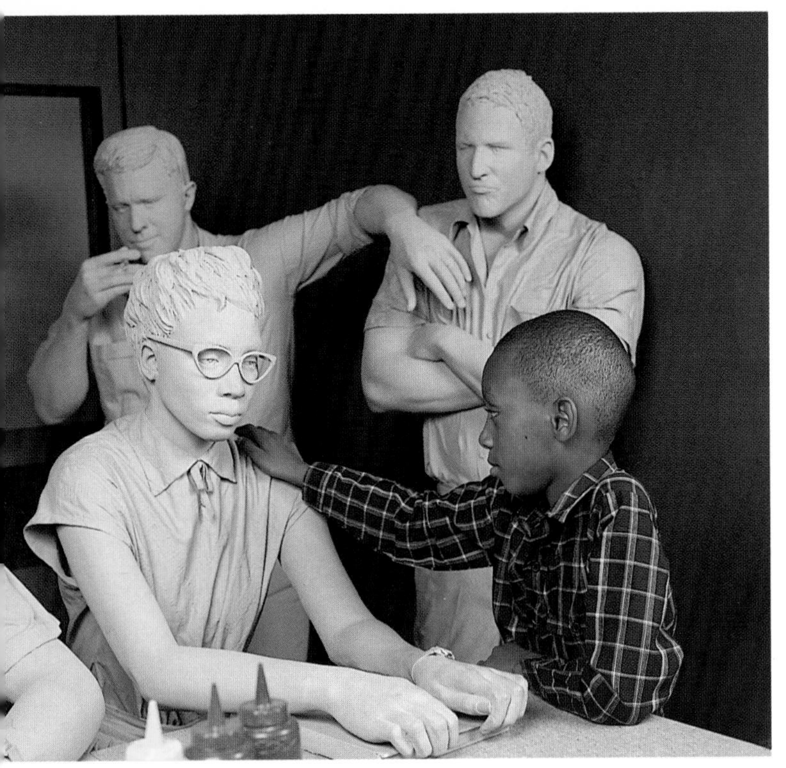

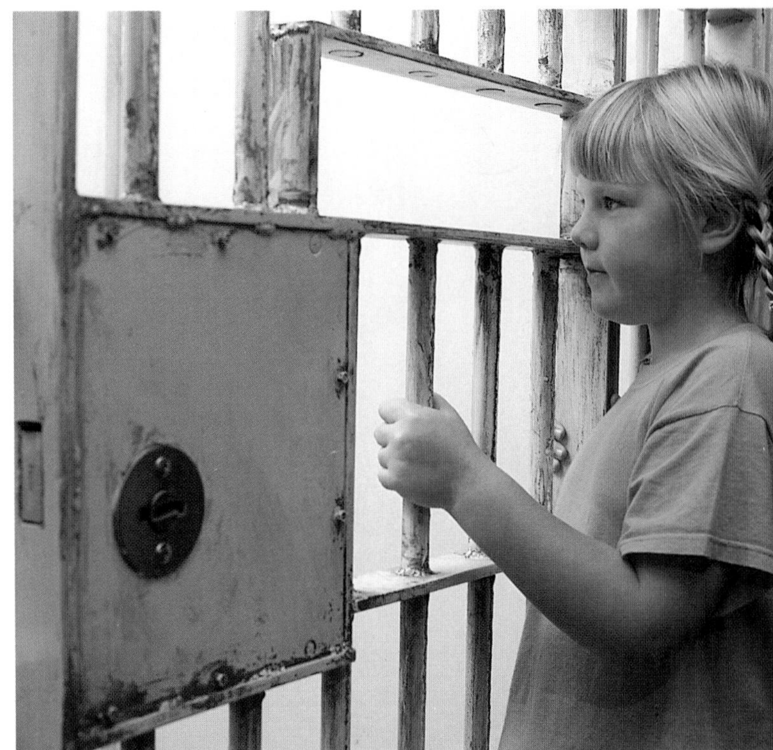

Visitors stand before the Sit-in exhibit and a replica of a Birmingham jail cell.

Visitors discover that the main exhibits in the museum capture the sounds, actions, and feelings of the period between 1954 and 1968. The exhibits are interactive, allowing guests to sit, touch, and listen. Thus, the Montgomery Bus Boycott exhibit permits you to hop on a bus and stand by a tired Rosa Parks, who fought for her rights by refusing to give up her seat to a white bus rider. Guests at the Student Sit-in exhibit hop onto a stool at a restored department-store lunch counter to view how college students were abused when they quietly protested for their right to be served in a public place. At the Freedom Riders exhibit, visitors can touch the outside of a badly burned Greyhound bus. The bus resembles those used in the dangerous 1961 Freedom Rides where people rode to protest segregated bus terminals.

During a tour of the National Civil Rights Museum, visitors can march with life-size protesters demanding voting rights, fair housing, and equal pay. They can stand before the Little Rock exhibit to view angry whites attempting to scare black students away from Central High School. Visitors can also feel what it is like to be in an Alabama jail cell like the one used to hold men, women, and children who marched for freedom in the city of Birmingham.

As the tour of the National Civil Rights Museum comes to an end, visitors walk through the Lorraine Motel until they reach the last exhibit—Rooms 306 and 307. Dr. Martin Luther King, Jr., was standing in front of Room 306 at the instant when he was shot. Room 307 was the room he occupied during his last stay at the motel. While visitors stand between these two rooms, they can read about the great leader's life and feel the power of the moment. In the background, gospel singer Mahalia Jackson croons her tender version of "Precious Lord," a slow and sorrowful tune that is often sung at funerals.

As Mahalia Jackson sings, visitors remember all that they have felt and seen during their tour of the National Civil Rights Museum. And suddenly everything comes together. We begin to understand that the civil rights movement in the United States was a struggle fought by everyday people like you and me. They were not rich, famous, or exceptional—just bold and determined to fight for freedom. The National Civil Rights Museum at the Lorraine Motel recreates their struggle, and we are left to carry the torch.

The museum provides newspapers from the movement and an opportunity to walk amid statues of marchers.

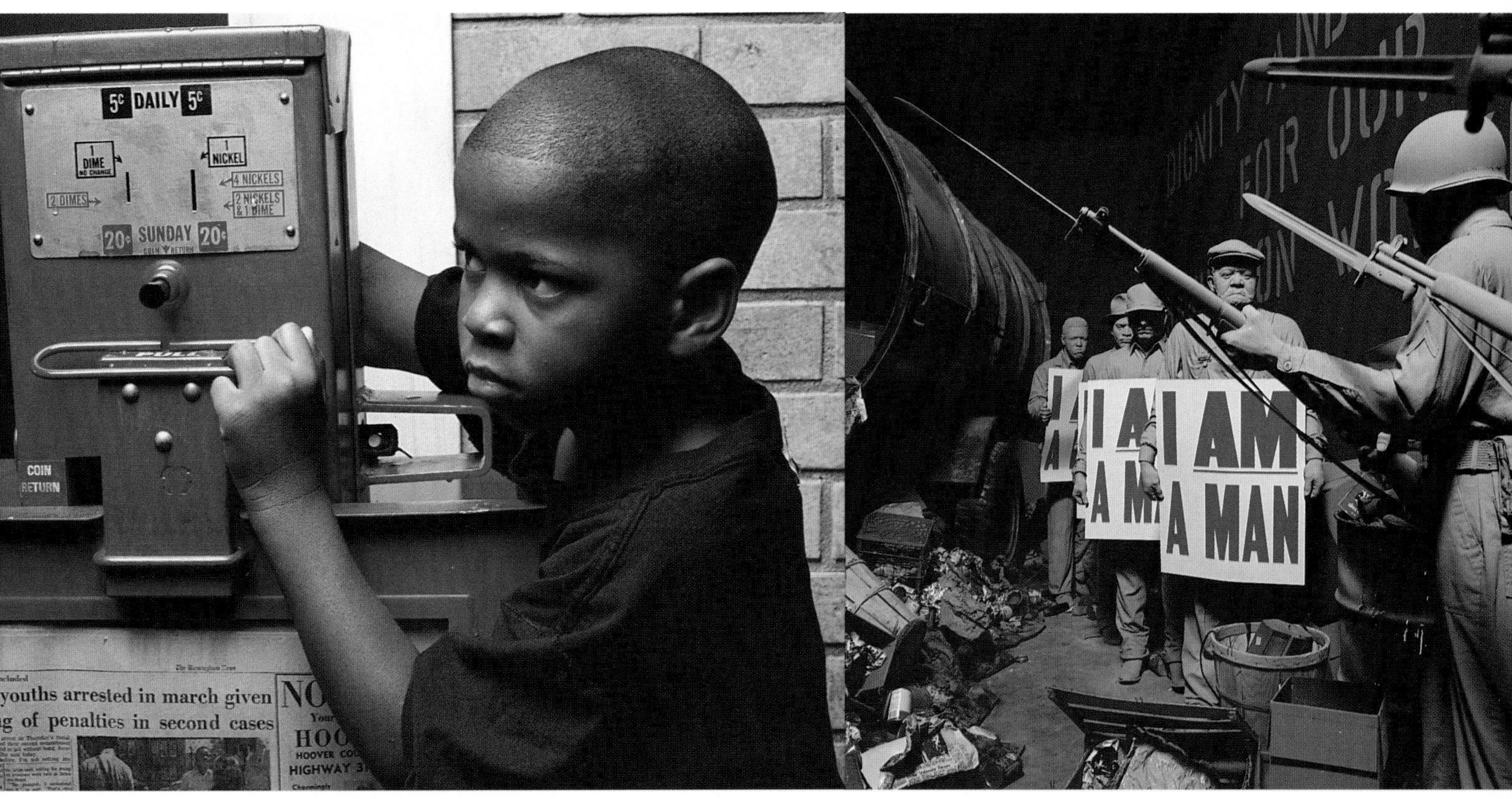

All aboard! Do you hear the engine roaring? Did people say that they were ready to ride? Then let's take a tour of the National Civil Rights Museum at the Lorraine Motel.

On this excursion, we will discover everyday people and learn about their efforts to fight against segregation and racial inequalities. They are heroes and heroines, though many of their names are unknown. History books do not tell who every one of them is. But because they stood for justice, the United States of America is a better place for all of us.

Today people of all races in America claim freedom. Blacks no longer have to enter through the back door of white-owned establishments. They no longer must drink from public water fountains with signs that read FOR COLORED ONLY. Because thousands of everyday people refused to remain second-class citizens, the races are no longer separate. Today we go to school together. We pray in the same houses of worship. Today we play on the same sports teams. We laugh. We talk. We go to the same parties. And friends are not turned away from our homes because they are a certain color.

Life in America has not always been this accepting. Before there was unity, there was strife. Before there was unity, there was struggle. A powerful movement had to happen. It was a movement conducted by ordinary men and women with everyday lives. No royalty. No riches. No fame. As we tour the National Civil Rights Museum, we will learn about their unyielding courage.

Young people have fun on a bus like the one that Rosa Parks rode.

WHY FIGHT TRAFFIC?
GO BY BUS

The first stop is the deep South: states such as Alabama, Georgia, Louisiana, Arkansas. During the 1950s, these and other southern states were known for their separation of the races. White and black people did not mingle with one another. This was called *segregation,* and it was the law in these states. For example, black home owners could buy houses only in all-black neighborhoods. Black students could go only to all-black schools, even if another school was closer. In restaurants, black citizens were seated in the rear beside the restaurant's kitchen. In public places like department stores, black shoppers could not use a rest room unless the sign on the door was marked COLORED.

Public transportation was a problem as well. When black riders boarded a bus, by law they had to take the farthest seat in the back. And if these riders found themselves sitting in the front, they were expected to give their seat away to any white person standing.

Students have been known to vandalize the statue of the bus driver who shouted at Rosa Parks.

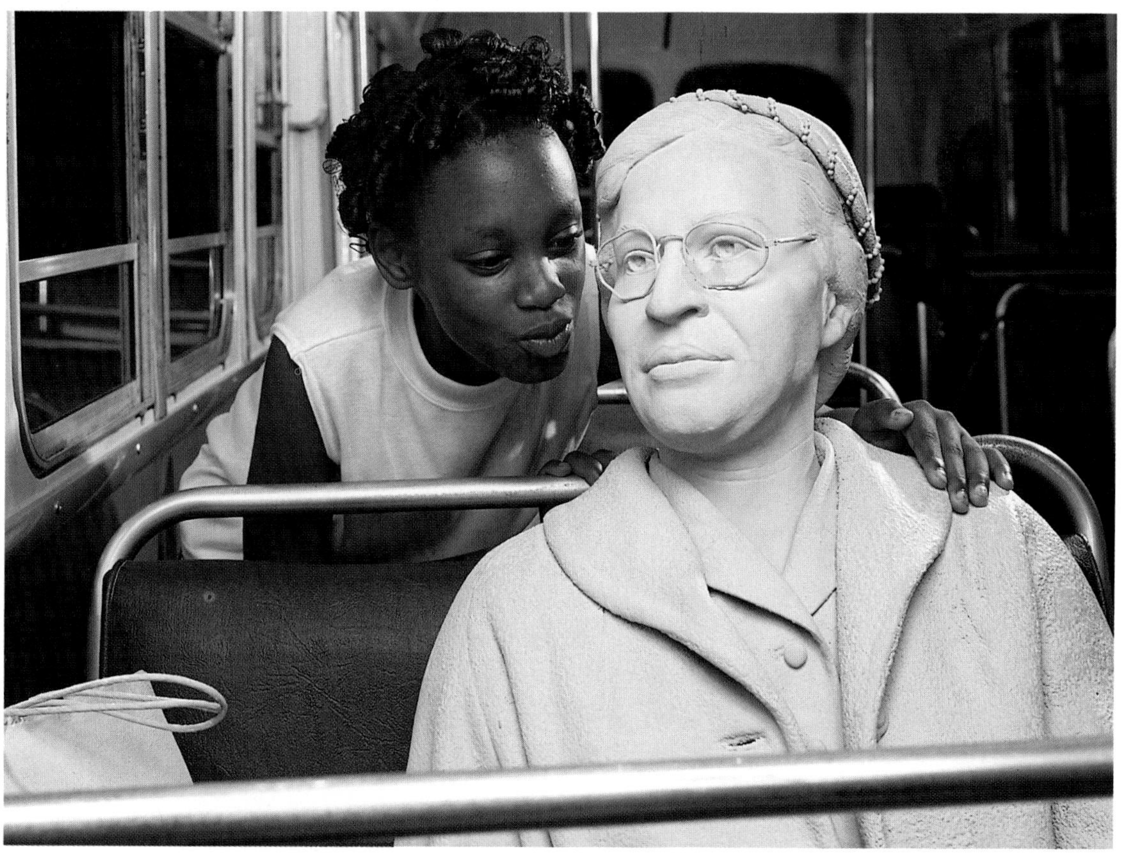

Young visitor whispers her thanks to a statue of Rosa Parks.

In the 1950s, public transportation was the cheapest way to get around town. Black Americans rode the buses daily. For a small fee, local transportation would take them all across the city. But the emotional price they had to pay was no small matter. Bus drivers were permitted to speak to adult black riders as if they were children. "Get up, girl!" they would shout. "Get up, boy!" And at that moment, black bus riders were supposed to stand and give away their seats.

In the fall of 1955, a proud woman named Rosa Parks had seen and suffered as much humiliation as she was willing to take. She was an everyday person, just like you. Her husband was a barber. She worked as a seamstress, and she was tired. She was tired of cruel bus drivers and segregation laws that did not make sense. So Mrs. Parks decided that something had to change.

She demanded justice, and the Montgomery Bus Boycott exhibit celebrates her bravery. Visitors bear witness as a life-size statue of a bus driver shouts out orders to the seated statue of a weary Rosa Parks, who refuses to take her "proper place" at the back of the bus.

The date was December 1, 1955. The place was Montgomery, Alabama— a southern town where Rosa Parks worked in a department store. After work that day, Mrs. Parks boarded a city bus to ride home. There was a seat available in the middle of the bus, and she sat in it. As other riders boarded, the white bus driver ordered Mrs. Parks to give her seat to a white man who was standing. She ignored the driver and kept her seat. Her rage had reached its limit. And because she stood up for her rights, the bus driver had her arrested.

At the police station, she had her fingerprints taken like a criminal. On December 5, she was convicted and fined ten dollars plus court fees. When details of the arrest became public, a group of black women—the Women's Political Council—took action. They asked ministers and civic leaders to help organize a boycott against the Montgomery City Lines bus company. One of the ministers to answer their call was twenty-six-year-old Dr. Martin Luther King, Jr.

Under the leadership of Dr. King, the black citizens of Montgomery held their bus boycott from December 5, 1955 to December 20, 1956. For over a year, black men, women, and children did not ride city buses. Instead, they formed car pools with neighbors or fellow church members. They rode in taxis that charged less than regular rates. And if they could not form a car pool or take a taxi, they walked.

Through the boycott, black citizens demanded courteous treatment by bus operators. They wanted to be seated on a first-come, first-served basis. They also demanded that blacks be allowed to apply for jobs as bus drivers. Dr. King presented these demands to city leaders, who did not take any action. And so the case was taken to the highest court in the United States.

The Supreme Court examined the Montgomery case and ruled that segregation on Alabama buses was unconstitutional. So, in December of 1956, Dr. King, Rosa Parks, and other black citizens of Montgomery paid their fares and rode the city buses once again. And this time, they sat wherever they pleased!

***Top:* Rosa Parks rides the city bus after the Supreme Court decision.**
***Bottom:* Rosa Parks is fingerprinted in a Montgomery jail for refusing to give up her seat.**

Our next stop is the Little Rock exhibit. The year was 1957. Although the Supreme Court had ruled that black and white children should go to the same public schools, they were still not doing so.

In Little Rock, nine teenagers were to be the first black students to attend all-white Central High School. Their attendance meant that the school would be integrated, with blacks and whites part of the same student body. To discourage the black students from entering the building, Governor Orval Faubus posted members of the Arkansas National Guard outside the school. Taking their cue from the governor, mobs of angry white citizens hurled insults and threats at the students.

To stop the unruly mobs from disrupting procedures to integrate Central High, President Dwight D. Eisenhower sent federal troops to escort the nine black students inside the school. Thus, Eisenhower became the first president in the post–Civil War era to use armed soldiers to support the rights of black Americans.

Students in front of the statue of Governor Faubus take notes on the Little Rock exhibit.

Visitors watch original Little Rock Nine news footage.

The black students assigned to Central High came to be known as the Little Rock Nine. They were Minniejean Brown, Elizabeth Eckford, Ernest Green, Thelma Mothershed, Melba Pattillo, Gloria Ray, Terrance Roberts, Jefferson Thomas, and Carlotta Walls.

On the September day that the Little Rock Nine were to enter Central High, Elizabeth Eckford did not get the message that she was to ride to school with the others. Instead, this brave girl faced a shouting white mob alone. According to witnesses, the mob was on its way to attack Elizabeth when a white woman quickly led her to safety.

Even after the federal troops arrived in Little Rock to escort the students onto their new campus, things did not calm down. The Little Rock Nine were still harassed by students and parents. Minniejean Brown was moved to pour chili on a white boy who called her vulgar names. Brown was suspended. Several weeks later, she was expelled from the school because she exchanged insults with a white girl.

White students shout insults as Elizabeth Eckford enters Central High School.

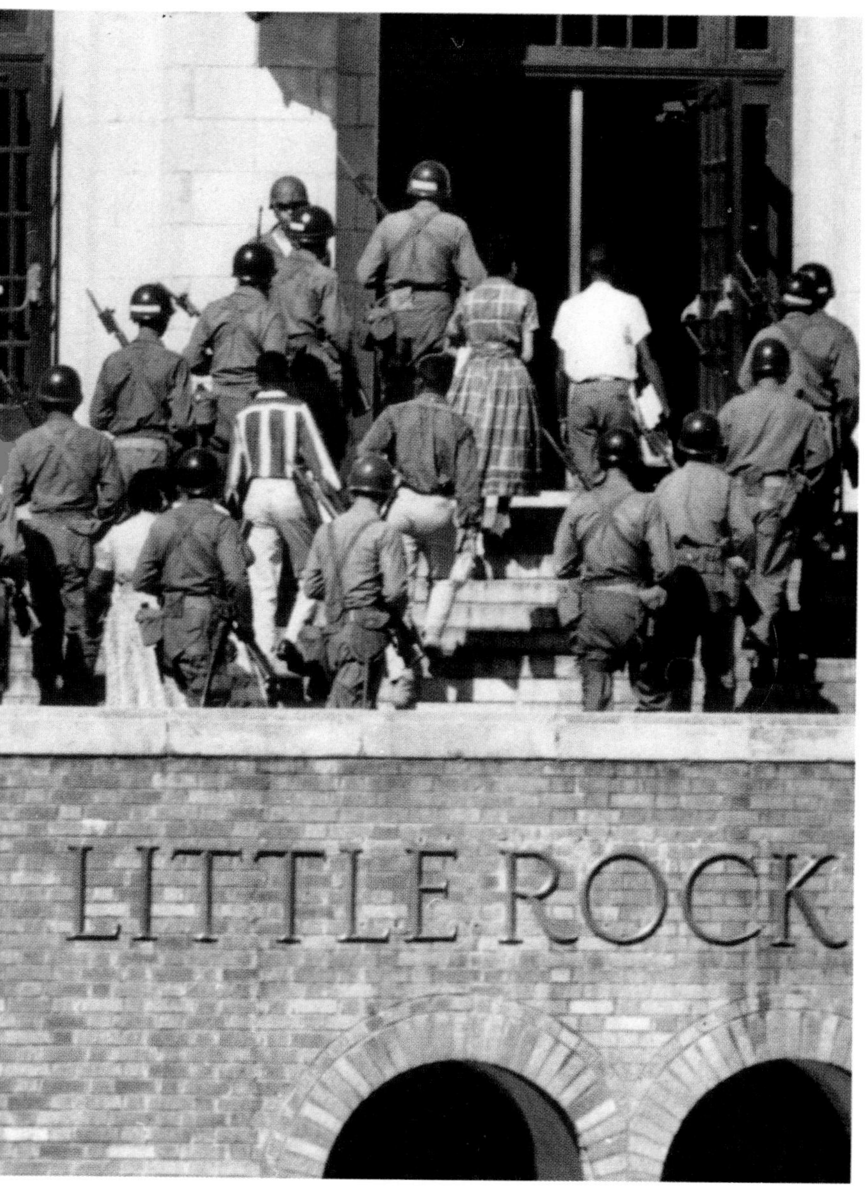

Left: **Federal troops escort black students to class.**
Right: **Ernest Green graduates from Central High.**

Of the nine students, Ernest Green was the only one to graduate from Central High School. "After I got that diploma," he said, "that was it. I had accomplished what I had come there for."

Just like you, Ernest Green and the Little Rock Nine were everyday people with dreams and ambitions. Like you, they wanted to learn. They wanted an equal opportunity to attend a decent school with up-to-date books and facilities. They integrated Central High and became living proof of the constitutional right of all Americans—no matter what the color of their skin—to a quality education.

After the Little Rock conflict, young people in America grew restless for change. In particular, college students were ready to make freedom a reality for all men, women, and children in the nation. To do this, they were prepared to fight and risk their lives. Their weapons of choice, however, were not fists or guns. In the 1960s, these young people chose to bring about change through nonviolent protests. Like Dr. Martin Luther King, Jr., and the black citizens of Montgomery, young people led boycotts. The student "sit-ins," as they were called, became one of the most popular and most effective forms of nonviolent protest in the '60s.

To conduct a sit-in, the students first identified stores that did not serve black customers at their lunch counters. Then they would take seats at these counters and ask to order. Black students were denied service because of segregation. When this happened, the students immediately informed the waiter and manager of the store that they would not move from their seats until fair treatment was given to black customers.

Students did not laugh or talk to one another during these protests. And when white customers came along to pour salt, ashes, and food on their heads, the students did not become violent. They simply took the abuse and remained in their seats, day after day.

The protesting students came so often and stayed so long that the segregated lunch counters suffered financially. The sit-ins were, therefore, effective. And they proved an important point: Young people had the power to change things.

Visitors sit at a lunch counter like the one where student protests began.

The National Civil Rights Museum documents the one student sit-in that began a wave of nonviolent protests all over the nation. This great sit-in took place in Greensboro, North Carolina, at the lunch counter of a Woolworth store.

Black students from North Carolina Agricultural and Technical College in Greensboro started the protest because they were upset over segregation and the mistreatment of black Americans. When the students began on February 1, 1960, they were determined to sit at the counter daily until the business changed its policies and served black customers with the same respect that it served whites.

Whites pour sugar, salt, and mustard over the heads of lunch counter demonstrators.

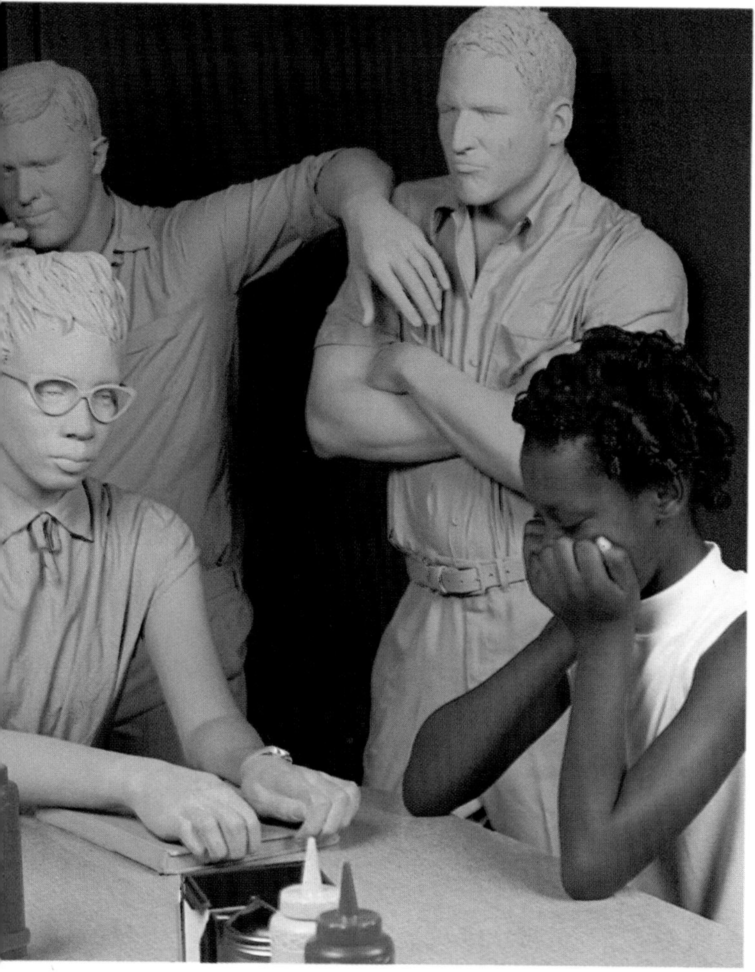

The Sit-in exhibit evokes feelings of struggle and strife.

During the first days of the sit-in, only black students participated. But by February 5, 1960, hundreds of black and white students sat together. According to their code, they were to enter the Woolworth neatly dressed. They were friendly at all times, though they were not treated in kind. Hecklers would often harass them, yet the harassment did not cause the protesters to give up their fight. They held on to the dream. They sat in day after day, and by July 1960, stores all over Greensboro were serving black and white customers at their lunch counters.

Following the Greensboro sit-ins, students extended their protests beyond lunch counters to restaurants, hotels, parks, swimming pools, and jobs. Student protests stretched across the country. From New York to Nashville, these college students were ordinary people who wanted to make a difference. So they did.

After the successful integration of lunch counters, young people moved on to desegregate interstate bus terminals. This was accomplished through what are remembered as the 1961 Freedom Rides.

The Congress of Racial Equality (CORE) and the Student Nonviolent Coordinating Committee (SNCC) were the two groups responsible for organizing students for the Freedom Rides that began in May 1961. During the dangerous trips, black and white members would board buses to travel together throughout the South. Their unity was the key to destroying segregation and unlawful practices directed against black travelers. These students had a clear purpose: They rode for freedom.

***Left:* A bruised Freedom Rider.**
***Right:* Freedom Riders nap in a Birmingham bus terminal.**

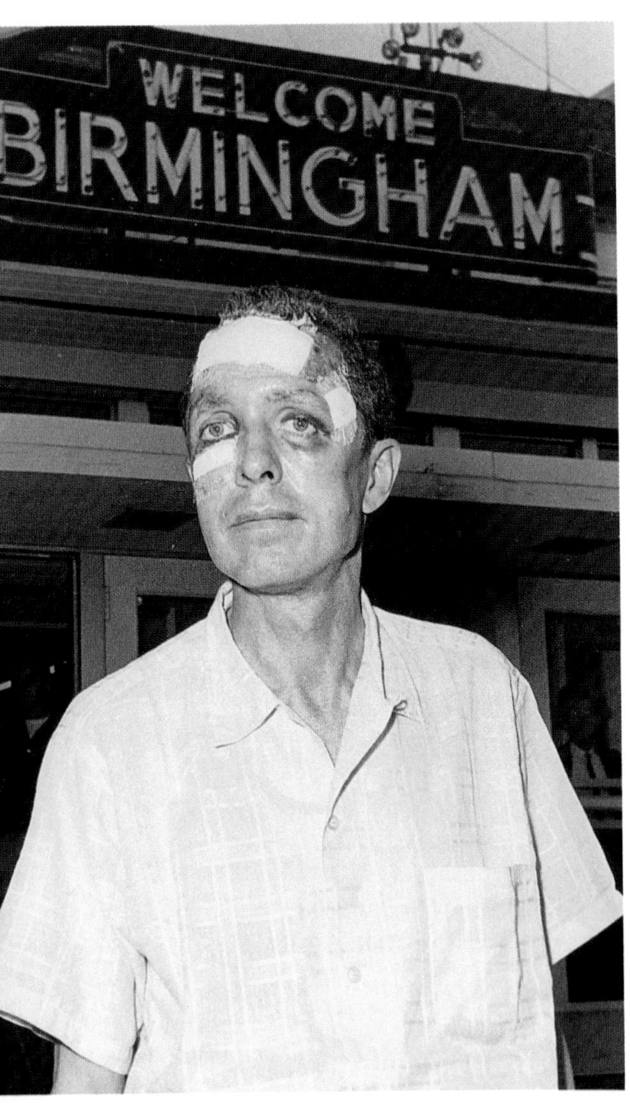

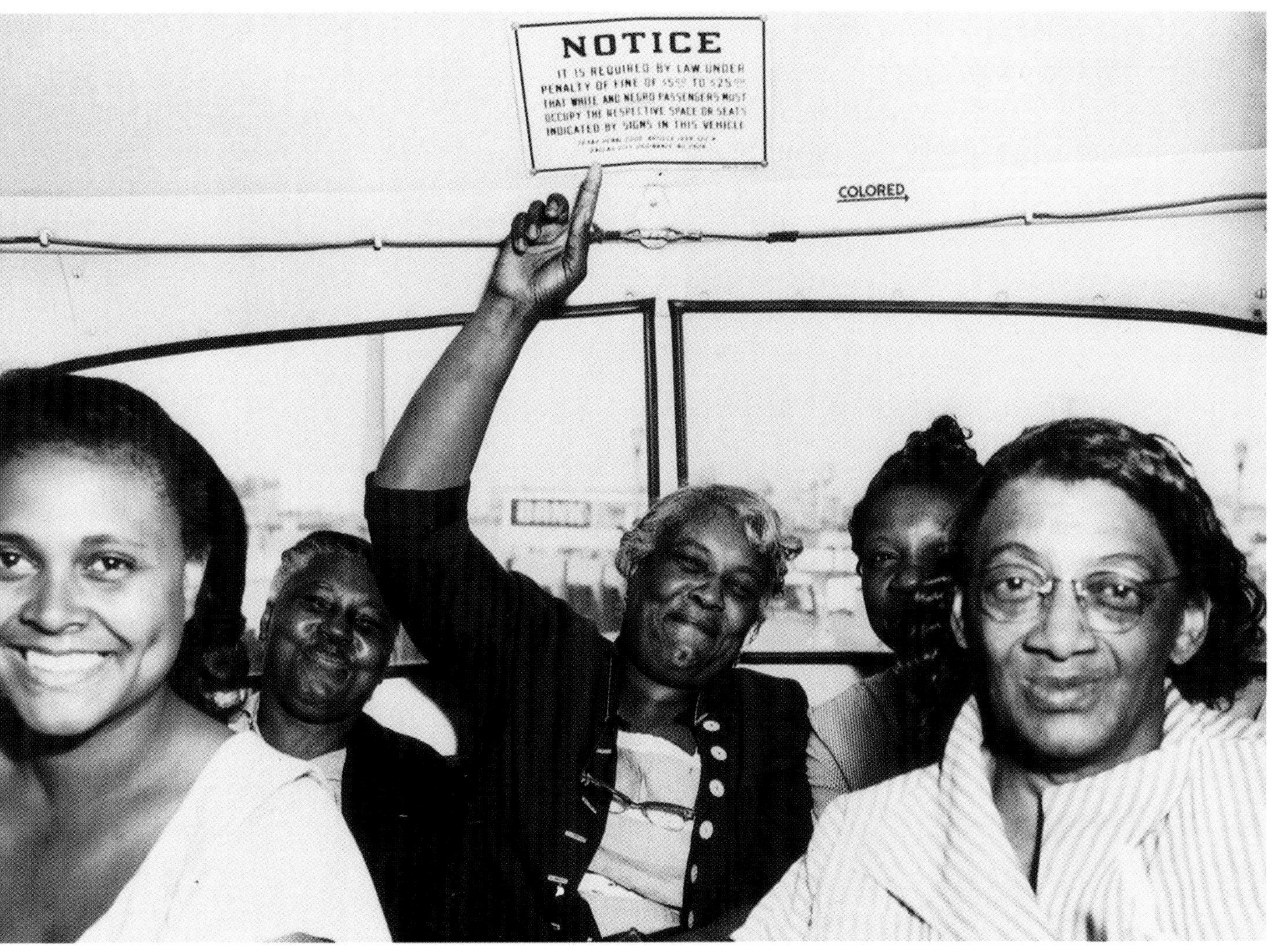

Passenger points to a segregation sign that is about to be torn down.

While on their journey, the Freedom Riders encountered stark violence and often came close to losing their lives. Angry mobs would identify their buses and flatten all the tires or set fire to the buses. These mobs also boarded the buses with planks and chains to beat the riders. Sometimes the traveling protesters were left sitting for days in cold bus terminals because bus drivers refused to drive them.

The Freedom Rides continued throughout the summer of 1961. The determined students would not let their will be broken. Though the government tried to convince them to stop riding—the trips were becoming more and more dangerous—the members of CORE and SNCC rode on! Then, in September of that same year, their efforts paid off: The Interstate Commerce Commission ended segregation in interstate bus terminals.

At the National Civil Rights Museum, visitors can stand before a Greyhound bus similar to the one that was burned outside of Anniston, Alabama, during the 1961 Freedom Rides. Visitors can see the charred, twisted metal and the gutted windows. It is a sight of terror, meant to remind people that hundreds of college students risked their lives so that all Americans can now travel in comfort.

Like you, the young Freedom Riders came from all over the nation. Some came from New York, Tennessee, Massachusetts, and Kansas. Others came from Illinois, Alabama, Georgia, Texas, and Washington, D. C. They were all colors and all religions. They suffered together. They committed themselves to the civil rights struggle when the United States government begged them to quit.

But the students did not quit. Together, they rode on to victory.

A badly burned Greyhound bus resembles the one destroyed in Anniston, Alabama.

Negro youths arrested in march given warning of penalties in second cases
NOW OPE
HOOVER A&
A&P
The Birmingham News
Birmingham Post-Herald

The next stop is Birmingham, Alabama. The year was 1963. Dr. Martin Luther King, Jr., and a group of black ministers who worked together in the Southern Christian Leadership Conference (SCLC) were busy planning a huge list of nonviolent activities in the city. The ministers titled their big event Project "C," for "confrontation."

Project "C" was an attempt to desegregate public facilities and increase employment of black Americans in commerce and industry. To accomplish these goals, Dr. King and the SCLC planned mass marches, sit-ins, and boycotts of downtown businesses.

At the time, Theophilus Eugene "Bull" Connor was the public safety commissioner of Birmingham. He requested that the courts order Dr. King and his followers not to march in the city. Connor let them know that if they did, they would go to jail. Dr. King and his followers ignored this order and marched. And as Bull Connor had promised, they were arrested quickly.

On May 2, Dr. King and his followers marched again to protest segregation and limited employment opportunities for black citizens. Close to one thousand protesters supported Dr. King on this march. And again they, too, were arrested. Hundreds of youths went to jail.

The following day saw more protests. Close to two thousand people marched. Adults came with their children; college students came with their friends. It was a protest group of all ages.

As the marchers turned a corner, Public Safety Commissioner Connor ordered them to turn around. They refused and kept marching. Then an awful thing happened. Connor ordered firefighters to spray the protesters with big fire hoses powerful enough to rip bark from a tree. The high-pressure hoses pushed people's bodies against buildings and cars. To create more confusion and injury, police dogs were ordered to attack innocent marchers. As people fought for their lives, the rest of the nation witnessed their terror on the evening news and on the front pages of newspapers.

Top: **Attack dogs and fire hoses were just two tactics used to stop marchers in Birmingham.**
Bottom: **Visitors come to know the fear of protesters during the Project "C" demonstrations.**

Dr. Martin Luther King, Jr., peers between the bars of his jail cell.

After Dr. King's first arrest during Project "C" in Birmingham, some white ministers in the city made public statements that criticized the civil rights movement and its leader. The ministers called Dr. King and his followers "impatient." They called the marching "unwise and untimely." And they suggested that Dr. King and his followers should not fight for freedom, but wait for the local and federal governments to solve their problems.

Dr. King read about the ministers' statements while in jail. Immediately he was moved to write a response. He had to let them know why black citizens could not be silent and wait for the government—politicians had been slow to bring about change. So from his cell, with a single lightbulb hanging overhead, Dr. King wrote a letter that explained his followers' position and feelings.

I guess it is easy for those who have never felt the stinging darts of segregation to say, "Wait." But when you have seen vicious mobs lynch your mothers and fathers at will and drown your sisters and brothers at whim; when you have seen hate-filled policemen curse, kick, brutalize, and even kill your black brothers and sisters . . . then you will understand why we [black Americans] find it difficult to wait. There comes a time when the cup of endurance runs over, and men are no longer willing to be plunged into an abyss of injustice.

Because jail did not offer the luxury of adequate light and a typewriter, Dr. King wrote his letter in tiny handwriting on scraps of paper. His lawyer, Arthur Shores, then secretly carried it out of jail in a worn brown briefcase. With the passing of time, Dr. King's "Letter from a Birmingham Jail" has become a classic example of protest literature.

A youngster gets acquainted with the kind of place where Dr. King wrote his famous letter.

A young man kneels on a glass-littered sidewalk across the street from the ruins of the 16th Street Baptist Church.

A woman is rushed from the scene as a fire burns furiously in an all-black section of Birmingham, Alabama.

Dr. King and his followers continued to march in Birmingham. They continued to sit in, and they continued the boycott of businesses that did not treat black customers fairly. The protesters would not stop. Eventually business owners—desperate because they were losing customers and not making enough money to pay their bills—asked politicians to reach an agreement with Dr. King and his followers.

Under the agreements that were made, black Birmingham citizens were guaranteed desegregated lunch counters, rest rooms, sitting rooms, and drinking fountains in downtown department stores. They were also promised the development of a fair employment committee, along with the release of all the protesters who were still in jail.

When the white citizens of Birmingham heard about the agreements, many were happy for what the protesters had achieved. Others were upset. Several groups of angry whites showed their feelings by bombing houses, churches, cars, and businesses that belonged to blacks. This senseless violence prompted President John F. Kennedy to set the wheels in motion for what was to become the Civil Rights Act of 1964.

Youngsters sing songs of freedom, march for their rights, and go to jail.

At the National Civil Rights Museum, the Birmingham exhibit highlights the contributions of those adults and children who fought for change in Alabama. The exhibit documents their struggle and reveals that children in the city fought just as hard as the adults. These children were just like you. They were students with homework to do and tests to take. They were brave, they were bold, and they marched. They attended church meetings with Dr. King. They participated in sit-ins and in boycotts. They made a contribution to the movement, and, thanks to their efforts, Birmingham changed.

Like the adults who marched, the children in the movement also had to pay a price for their boldness and effort. They, too, were put in cold, crowded jail cells, and many of them were suspended from school because of their participation.

Students crowd into a holding cell like the ones where young protesters were kept.

Following the Birmingham experience, civil rights leaders banded together to plan a march on Washington, D. C., the nation's capital. The march had several purposes: It would demand that the government ensure voting rights for black citizens and equal access to decent housing, jobs, public accommodations, and top-quality schools. The march would be an attempt to gain economic and political freedom for all black citizens and to gain human rights for all of the nation's people who suffered from poverty and the lack of opportunity.

The March on Washington was held on Wednesday, August 28, 1963. People from around the country came to the Lincoln Memorial to participate in the event—black people, white people, young and old. Some had come by bus, some by train or plane. Others had traveled by car, while some had walked from their cities to the nation's capital. In all, over 250,000 protesters marched on Washington.

The weather was pleasant that day as several civil rights leaders delivered speeches and famous singers celebrated the moment with song. Finally Dr. Martin Luther King, Jr., was introduced.

When Dr. King moved to the microphone, the 250,000 protesters cheered with excitement. They applauded the great leader. They waved their protest signs high. Then Dr. King delivered to the nation his remarkable "I Have a Dream" speech, which continues to promote unity among the races.

> *So I say to you, my friends, that even though we must face the difficulties of today and tomorrow, I still have a dream. It is a dream deeply rooted in the American dream that one day this nation will rise up and live out the true meaning of its creed. . . . I have a dream that one day, every valley shall be exalted, every hill and mountain shall be made low, the rough places shall be made plain, and the crooked places shall be made straight . . . and all flesh shall see it together.*

An aerial view of the Lincoln Memorial, where 250,000 protesters marched for their rights on August 28, 1963.

Young boy mounts podium, while others stand amid statues of photojournalists at the exhibit.

The March on Washington was so large and included so many people from different walks of life that photographers for newspapers and magazines were sent to Washington to take pictures. All the major television networks sent reporters and camera crews to report stories. Thus, people across the nation were able to witness the power of that day in print and on television.

Dr. King delivers his stirring "I Have a Dream" speech.

Top: **Students display their own protest signs at the March on Washington exhibit.**
Bottom: **Leaders of the March on Washington lock arms as thousands protest for their rights.**

When people think about the March on Washington, they recall the protesters and a sea of waving signs. There were thousands and thousands of signs. Some were homemade; some were printed. Some were big; some were small. Yet they all had one thing in common. Each sign made a demand for justice. They contained messages, such as WE DEMAND DECENT HOUSING! WE DEMAND JOBS NOW! WE DEMAND AN END TO POLICE BRUTALITY! WE DEMAND VOTING RIGHTS!

All of these issues were important to protesters because black Americans did not enjoy the comfortable lifestyle that many white Americans enjoyed. In the workplace, black Americans were paid less money than white Americans. In the world of politics, many black Americans were kept from voting. And in housing, black Americans were often forced to live in slums even when they had the money to move to a better place.

Marchers carried their signs to Washington to bring equality to all people. One year later, they came to see the positive results of their labor. President Lyndon B. Johnson signed the Civil Rights Act of 1964. This act outlawed discrimination on the job. It outlawed discrimination in public places. It ordered the desegregation of schools and outlawed discrimination on the basis of sex.

With the passing of this new act, however, there was no room to rest easy. Other changes were in store. So the protesters gathered their signs and moved on to continue their fight for justice.

President Lyndon B. Johnson shakes hands with Dr. King and offers his pen after signing the Civil Rights Act.

Several boys walk across replica of the Edmund Pettus Bridge while keeping an eye on looming statues of state troopers.

The next exhibit at the National Civil Rights Museum documents the march from Selma to Montgomery in Alabama. This event began on March 7, 1965. It was a Sunday, windy and cool. Over five hundred men, women, and children prepared for another protest. They would walk from Selma to the state capital, where they were to tell Governor George Wallace that it was time for black citizens to receive full voting rights in Alabama. Montgomery was about fifty miles away from Selma, so protesters carried bedrolls and bags of food on their backs. They prepared themselves for a long journey as they proceeded out of Brown's Chapel Methodist Church.

Governor Wallace warned protesters not to march. He told them that they would be stopped, but they marched on, anyway. They marched to gain voting rights for black citizens in Alabama.

When the hundreds of marchers reached the Edmund Pettus Bridge in East Selma, which led the way to Montgomery, they were met by a terrible surprise. On the other side of the bridge, state troopers with nightsticks, whips, and gas masks were waiting to stop the march. Protesters, however, kept marching. Like the protesters in Selma, museum guests can walk over a replica of the Edmund Pettus Bridge, the beginning of the journey to Alabama's state capital.

Major John Cloud asked the protesters to return to Brown's Chapel for their safety. He asked them to go home, but no one turned back. So Major Cloud ordered his men to advance. Immediately the troopers rushed into the protesters and began an attack with their nightsticks and fists. Children began to cry. Adults began to scream, and in the middle of all the drama, protesters were bombed with tear gas. The tear gas was so thick that it covered the street like a dense blanket of fog.

This day in American history came to be known as "Bloody Sunday." It is significant because, after President Johnson witnessed the protesters and their suffering, he committed himself to ending all practices that denied people their right to vote. On August 6, President Johnson signed the Voting Rights Act of 1965. This act ensured that all black citizens, all poor citizens, and all non-English-speaking citizens could exercise their right to vote in local and national elections. A brand-new day was on the horizon.

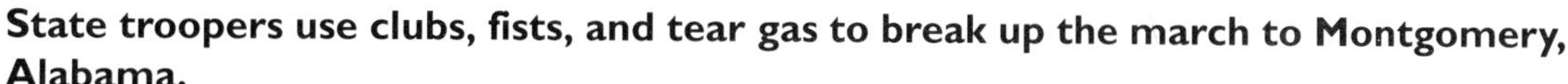

State troopers use clubs, fists, and tear gas to break up the march to Montgomery, Alabama.

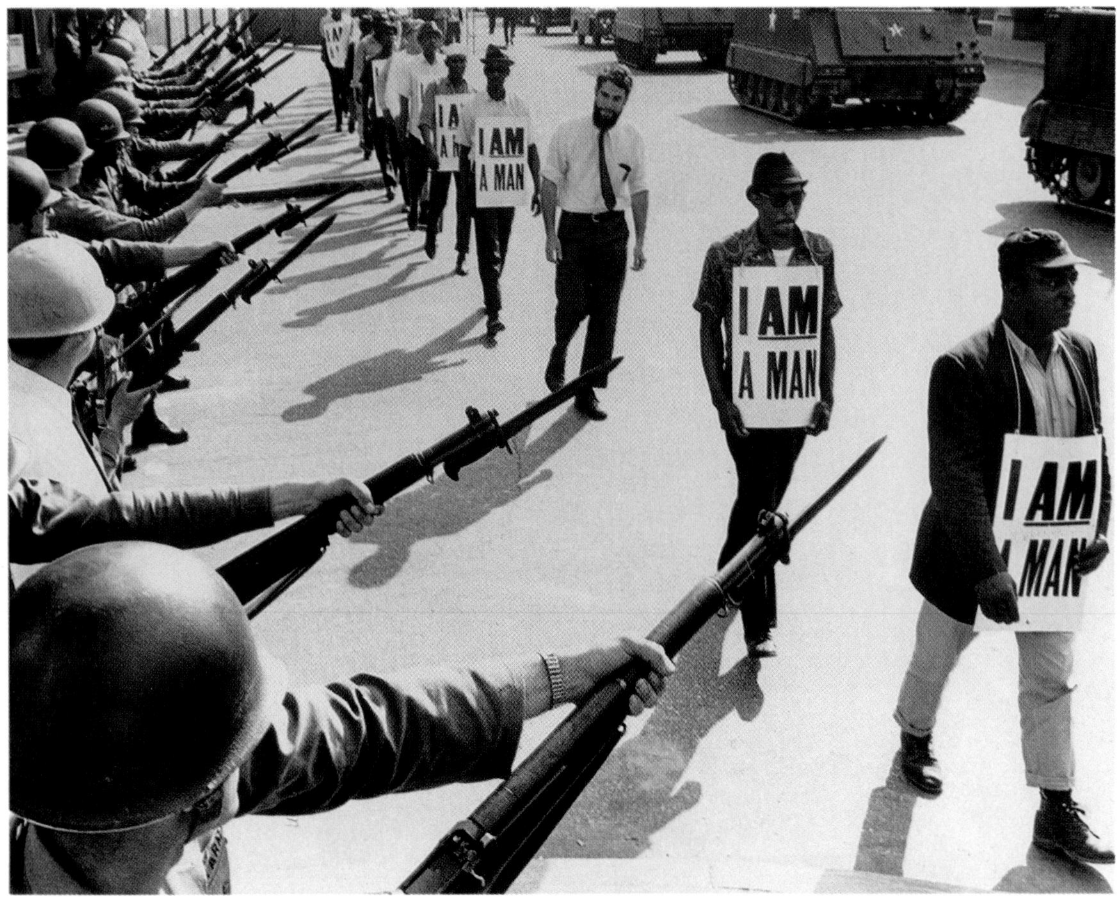

National Guardsmen use bayonets to block Beale Street in Memphis as protesters march.

Following the Voting Rights Act of 1965, black Americans throughout the South registered to vote. Then they went to exercise their new voting power, electing black politicians to several local and national offices. This proved that the United States was clearly taking steps toward justice and equality. However, the stubborn city of Memphis, Tennessee, still tried its hardest not to change. The National Civil Rights Museum documents this historical period.

The year was 1968, and black sanitation workers in Memphis were on strike because white city leaders refused to recognize their union and their demands for an increase in pay. The museum exhibit reveals that these strikers wore big, boldly printed signs that read I AM A MAN, to show that they were proud and would not settle for injustice. To help the workers obtain better wages, Dr. Martin Luther King, Jr., came to Memphis and organized a protest march. The march was not successful because it was interrupted by looting and rioting.

During the first protest, Dr. King did not accomplish anything for the striking workers, but he was determined to help their cause. So he returned to Memphis and stayed at the Lorraine Motel, where he prepared for a second march. After all, these men were hard workers. Their jobs were important to the entire city, and they deserved better wages.

Memphis sanitation workers were determined to win better wages through nonviolent protests.

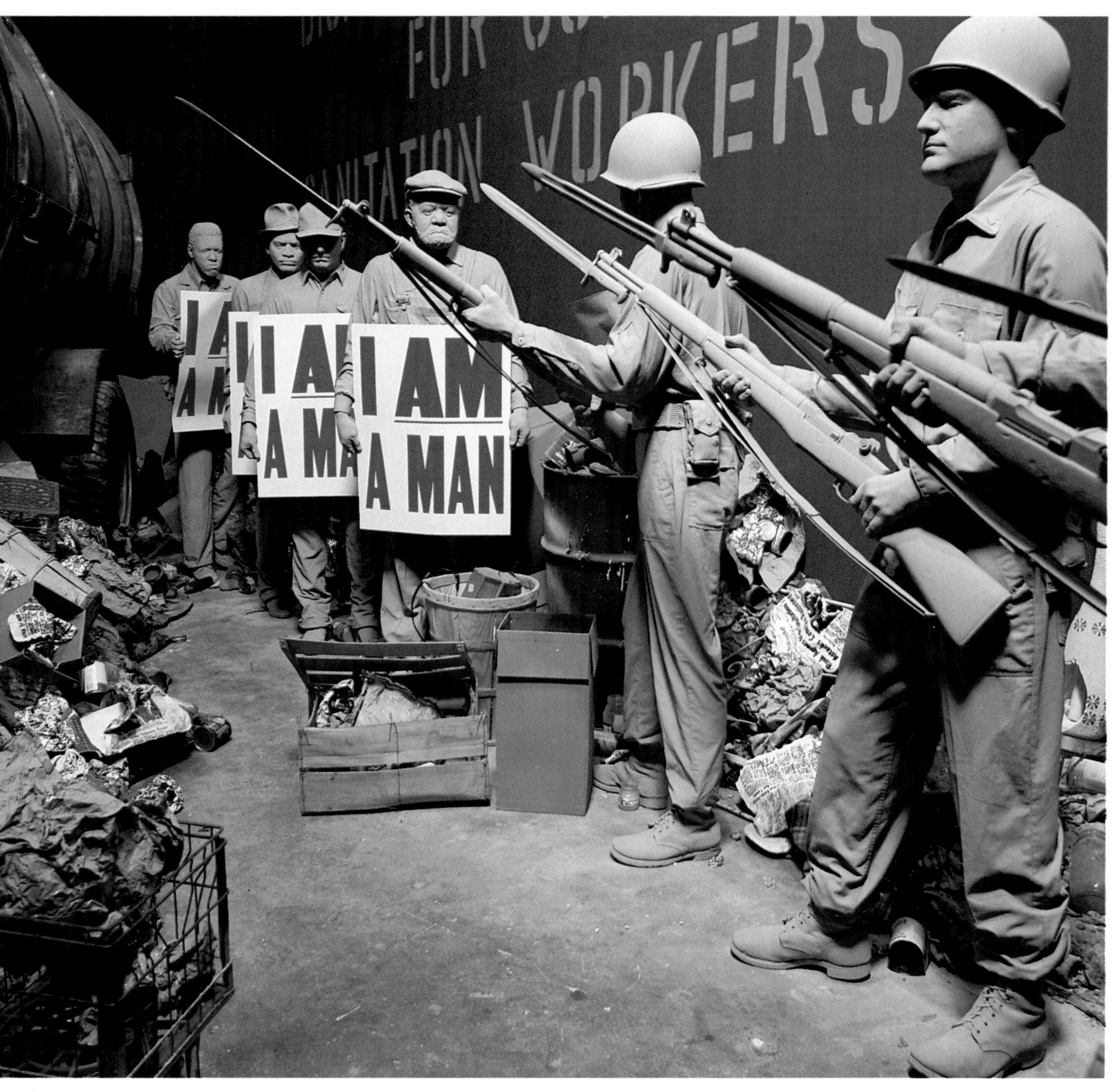

When Dr. King returned to Memphis on April 3, he checked into Room 307 at the Lorraine Motel and met with several black sanitation workers, reporters, and several staff members from the SCLC who were helping to coordinate the march. Later, during the evening, he went to Mason Temple to speak with the people who would participate in the march. Dr. King encouraged them to conduct a peaceful protest, and to walk in the spirit of love and nonviolence. He also asked that they not grow weary or give up on their efforts, for America was changing, and justice would be achieved just as he dreamed. He asked the audience to do whatever was necessary to help the movement.

> *Let us develop a kind of dangerous unselfishness. Let us rise up tonight with a greater readiness. Let us stand with a greater determination. And let us move on in these powerful days, these days of challenge to make America what it ought to be.*

While on the journey for freedom, Dr. King received numerous death threats. To prepare his followers, family, and friends for the possibility of his passing, Dr. King told them all about the death threats and said that they did not scare him—he was willing to sacrifice his life for the movement. He was ready and willing to die for freedom.

The National Civil Rights Museum at the Lorraine Motel stands in downtown Memphis, Tennessee.

After his speech at Mason Temple, Dr. King never led another march. He never preached another sermon or spoke to another band of followers, because on April 4, 1968, he was assassinated. The nation's great dreamer was shot by a sniper's bullet while standing on the balcony of the Lorraine Motel. The time was 6 P.M., and, in that instant, many Americans feel that the greatest chapter in the civil rights movement died with the passing of Dr. King and his courageous spirit.

Although Dr. King had discussed his own death, this did not remove the shock of his assassination outside Room 306. The brutal murder shook the world. It left millions of people heartbroken. His friends the Reverends Ralph Abernathy, Jesse Jackson, Andrew Young, and Billy Kyles were especially shaken because they were at the motel when Dr. King was murdered.

He had been their great teacher. He had taught them how to organize protests. He had taught them how to win a fight for justice without the use of foul language, fists, or guns. Dr. King had taught them how to bring about change through love, and, like the rest of the world, they would miss him deeply.

Dr. Martin Luther King, Jr., on the balcony where, one day later, he would be slain. With him are Hosea Williams, Jesse Jackson, and Ralph Abernathy.

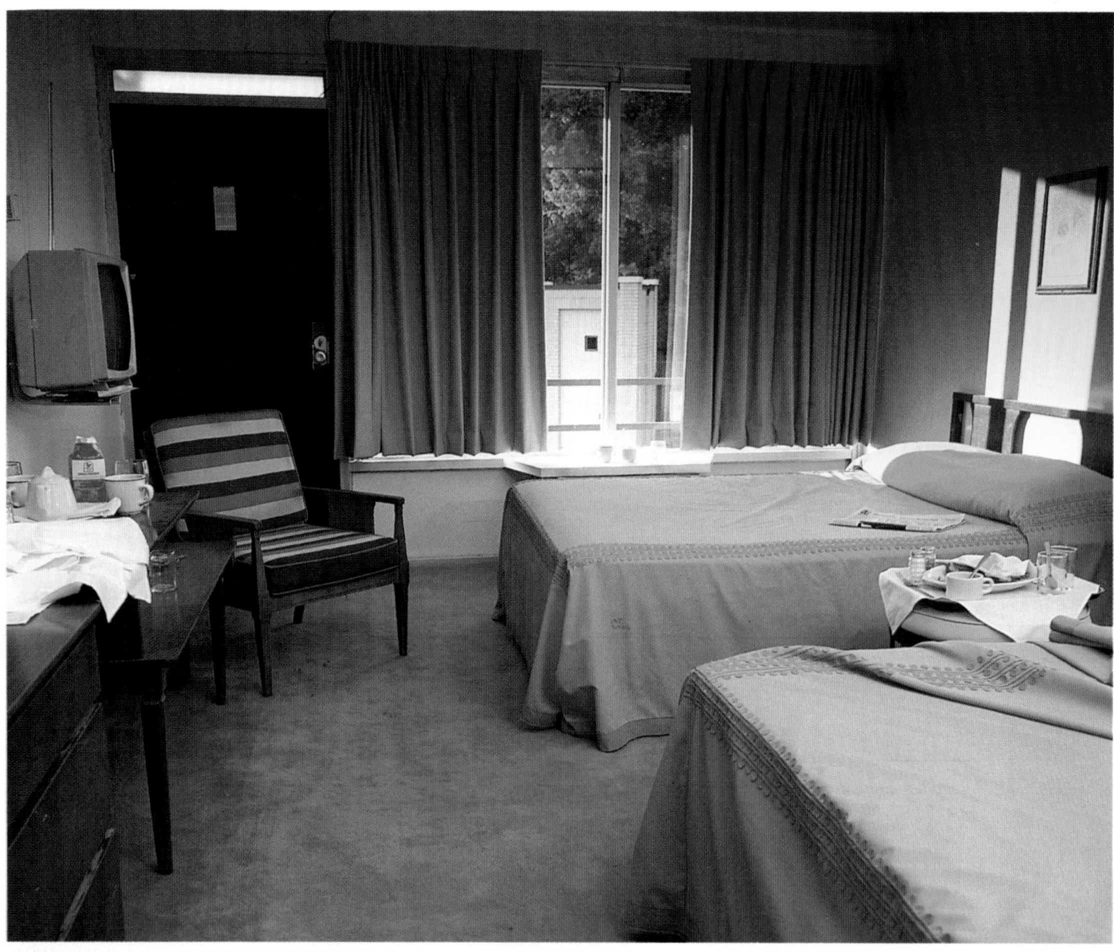

Dr. King was killed in front of Room 306, which has been made to look just as it did on the day of his death.

The last exhibit at the National Civil Rights Museum brings us inside the Lorraine Motel. The Lorraine's Rooms 306 and 307 are just as they were on the day of Dr. King's final visit. The curtains are open. There are empty coffee cups, drinking glasses, and used ashtrays sitting on the furniture. Between two beds in Room 307, visitors also see the last dinner that Dr. King shared with the Reverend Ralph Abernathy.

Outside Room 306, there is a white wreath that hangs on the balcony. People from all over the world come to see it. They take pictures of the wreath or sometimes they just stand before it and cry, for the wreath marks the very spot where America's great dreamer lost his life in the struggle for justice and equality.

When young people reach the last exhibit at the Lorraine Motel, they often ask, "Is the civil rights movement over now?" The answer is no. Our struggle continues because today we must work to end social problems like poverty and homelessness. We must work to stop police brutality and gang violence. We must fight to end racial prejudice, physical abuse, and all other forms of hatred.

Like the thousands of everyday people who walked with Dr. King, we must stand together in the spirit of unity. We must look around our world and try to correct the many wrongs that we see. Our road will not be easy, but we can do it. Like Rosa Parks, we can do it. Like the Little Rock Nine, we can do it. Like the Freedom Riders and the people of Selma, we can do it. Together we can make a difference. Then tomorrow's people will look upon our efforts and be inspired to do the same.

Youngsters stand together before *Movement to Overcome* and reflect on their visit to the museum.

The balcony then . . . and now.

CHRONOLOGY

1954 The Supreme Court declares that segregation in public schools is unconstitutional.

1955 Rosa Parks refuses to surrender her seat on the bus to a white rider and is arrested. Her protest inspires the Montgomery bus boycott.

1956 The Supreme Court rules segregation on Alabama buses unconstitutional.

1957 Dr. Martin Luther King, Jr., Bayard Rustin, and Stanley Levison form the Southern Christian Leadership Conference (SCLC) to achieve equality for black Americans through nonviolent protests.

1957 The Little Rock Nine integrate Central High School in Little Rock, Arkansas.

1960 Sit-ins in Greensboro, North Carolina, inspire students throughout the South to protest and boycott businesses that do not serve black Americans.

1961 CORE and SNCC begin freedom rides that lead to desegregation of interstate bus stations.

1961 Malcolm X founds *Muhamad Speaks*, the official publication of the Nation of Islam.

1963 Dr. Martin Luther King, Jr., is arrested during Project "C" demonstrations and writes his "Letter from a Birmingham Jail" to explain why black Americans must protest.

1963 Bayard Rustin and A. Philip Randolph, along with other civil rights leaders, organize the March on Washington to express the economic and political concerns of minorities.

1964 President Lyndon B. Johnson signs the Civil Rights Act, a milestone in the struggle for equality.

1964 Dr. Martin Luther King, Jr., is awarded the Nobel Peace Prize.

1964 Malcolm X leaves the Nation of Islam and becomes a leading spokesperson on racial pride. Founds the Organization of African-American Unity.

1965 Malcolm X is assassinated on February 21, 1965.

1965 State troopers attack protesters on the Edmund Pettus Bridge. Dr. Martin Luther King, Jr., and the Reverend Ralph Abernathy plan a march in Alabama from Selma to Montgomery to demand voting rights for black Alabama citizens.

1965 President Johnson signs the Voting Rights Act, ensuring that all black citizens could exercise their right to vote in local and national elections.

1967 SNCC becomes a militant group under the leadership of H. Rap Brown.

1968 Dr. Martin Luther King, Jr., arrives in Memphis, Tennessee, to organize a protest march of black sanitation workers. He delivers his final sermon at Mason Temple.

1968 Dr. Martin Luther King, Jr., is assassinated at the Lorraine Motel in Memphis, Tennessee. *In 1969 James Earl Ray was sentenced to ninety-nine years in jail for the murder of Dr. King.*

SUGGESTED FURTHER READING

Adams, Russell L. *Great Negroes Past and Present.* Chicago: Afro-Am Publishing Co., 1984. An encyclopedia of heroic and influential Africans and African Americans who have made various contributions to the world. (Ages 10-up)

Greene, Carol. *Thurgood Marshall: First African-American Supreme Court Justice.* Chicago: Children's Press, 1991. Biography of the first African American appointed to the Supreme Court. (Ages 5–9)

Haskins, James. *Outward Dreams: Black Inventors and Their Inventions.* New York: Bantam Books, 1992. Photographs and biographies of African-American men and women who changed the world with their inventions. (Ages 10-up)

Levine, Ellen. *Freedom's Children.* New York: Putnam, 1993. Photographs and narratives from children of the civil rights movement. (Ages 11-up)

———. *If You Lived at the Time of Martin Luther King.* New York: Scholastic, 1990. A general account of organizations and leaders that made the civil rights movement what it was. (Ages 7–12)

Myers, Walter Dean. *Now Is Your Time! The African-American Struggle for Freedom.* New York: HarperCollins, 1992. An overview of African-American history from slavery to the present. (Ages 10-up)

Parks, Rosa. *Rosa Parks: Mother to a Movement.* New York: Dial, 1992. An autobiography of the woman whose protest led to the Montgomery bus boycott. (Ages 11-up)

Plowden, Martha Ward. *Famous Firsts of Black Women.* Gretna, LA: Pelican Publishing Co., 1993. Includes famous African-American women from the worlds of sports, business, and the arts. (Ages 10-up)

Stein, Richard C. *The Montgomery Bus Boycott.* Chicago: Children's Press, 1993. A detailed discussion of the Montgomery bus boycott and the people who made it a success. (Ages 7–12)

Wilkinson, Brenda. *Jesse Jackson: Still Fighting for the Dream.* Englewood Cliffs, NJ: Silver Burdett Press, 1990. Biography of civil rights activist and politician who marched with Dr. King and continues to strive toward equal rights for all Americans. (Ages 10-up)

BIBLIOGRAPHY

Ebony Magazine. *Ebony Pictorial History of Black America.* 3 vols. Nashville, TN: The Southwestern Company, 1971.

Time-Life Books. *African American Voices of Triumph: Perseverance.* Foreword by Henry Louis Gates, Jr., Alexandria, Va: Time-Life Custom Publishing, 1993.

"Lorraine Motel Opens Its Doors Again." *Tennessee Teacher*. January 1992: 9–15.

Low, W. Augustus, and Virgil A. Clift, eds. "Civil Rights." In *Encyclopedia of Black America.* New York: Da Capo Press, 1984.

McKissack, Patricia, and Fred McKissack. *The Civil Rights Movement in America: From 1865 to the Present.* 2nd ed. Chicago: Children's Press, 1991.

Miller, Marilyn. *The Bridge at Selma.* Morristown, NJ: Silver Burdett Press, 1984.

Ploski, Harry A. and James Williams, eds. "Chronology: A Historical Review." In *The Negro Almanac: A Reference Work on the Afro-American.* New York: John Wiley & Sons, 1983.

Thomas, Keith. "Keeping the Dream." *Atlanta Constitution,* 30 June 1991, Section M, 1–6.

Thomas, William. "Building a Dream: Death of Dr. King Created an Indelible Mark Here." *Commercial Appeal,* Memphis, TN, 30 June 1991, Section G, 1–9.

Washington, James M., ed. *A Testament of Hope: The Essential Speeches and Writings of Martin Luther King, Jr.* New York: Harper & Row, 1986.

INDEX

Photographs are indicated in **boldface.**

Abernathy, Ralph, 50, **51,** 53
Anniston, Alabama, 28
Arkansas National Guard, 18

Bailey, Loree, 7
Bailey, Walter, 7
Birmingham, Alabama, 10, **30,** 31, 32, 35–36, **35, 36**
"Bloody Sunday," 45, **45**
bombings, **34,** 35, **35**
boycotts, 22, 31, 35, 36
Brown, Minniejean, 20
Brown's Chapel Methodist Church, 44, 45
bus terminals, 26, **26,** 27
bus travel, 26, 27, **27,** 28

Central High School, 10, 18, **19,** 20, **20,** 21, **21**
Civil Rights Act of 1964, 35, 43
  signing of, **43**
Cloud, John, 45
college students, role in civil rights movement of, 10, 22, 25, 26, 28, 31
Congress of Racial Equality (CORE), 26, 27
Connor, Theophilus Eugene "Bull," 31

desegregation
  in Birmingham, 31, 35
  of Central High School, 18, 20, 21, **21**
  of interstate bus terminals, 26–28, **26**
  of lunch counters, 22, 24–25, 35

Eckford, Elizabeth, 20, **20**
Edmund Pettus Bridge, 45
Eisenhower, Dwight D., 18

Faubus, Orval, 18, **18**
federal troops, intervention of, 20, **21,** 35
Freedom Ride bus, **28–29**
Freedom Riders, **26,** 27, **27,** 28
Freedom Rides, 10, 26, 27, 28

Green, Ernest, 20, 21, **21**
Greensboro, North Carolina, 24–25, **24**
Greyhound bus, 10, 28, **28–29**

I AM A MAN, **46,** 46
"I Have a Dream" speech, 39, **41**
Interstate Commerce Commission, 27

Jackson, Jesse, 50, **51**
Jackson, Mahalia, 11
Johnson, Lyndon B., 43, **43,** 45

Kennedy, John F., 35
King, Coretta Scott, 9
King, Martin Luther, Jr., 7, 8, 9, 22, **43**
  assassination of, 1, 7, 11, 50, 53
  in Birmingham, 31, 32–33, **32,** 35, 36
  death threats received by, 48, 50
  at the Lorraine Motel, 1, 48, 50, **51,** 53

at the March on Washington, 39, **41**
in Memphis, 46, 47–48
and the Montgomery bus boycott, 17
Kyles, Billy, 50

"Letter from a Birmingham Jail," 32–33
Lincoln Memorial, **38,** 39
Little Rock, Arkansas, 18, 20
Little Rock Nine, 20, **20,** 21, **21**
Lorraine Foundation, 9
Lorraine Motel, 1, **6,** 7–9, **8,** 11, 12, 47, 48, **48–49,** 50, **50, 51, 52,** 53, **53, 54**
celebrity guests at, 7
lunch counters, 10, 22, **22–23, 24,** 25, **25**

March on Washington, **38,** 39, 41, **42,** 43
Mason Temple, 48, 50
Memphis sanitation workers' strike, 47–48, **46**
Memphis, Tennessee, 1, 7, 46, **46,** 47, 48
Montgomery, Alabama, 17, 22, 44
Montgomery bus boycott, 15, 17
Mothershed, Thelma, 20

National Civil Rights Museum, 9–11, 12, **48–49, 50,** 51, **56**
exhibits at, **6, 9,** 10–11, **10, 11, 12–13, 14,** 15, **15,** 18, **18, 19, 22–23,** 24, **25,** 28, **28–29, 30, 33,** 36, **37, 40, 42,** 44, **44,** 45, 46, **47, 52,** 53, **53, 54–55**

nonviolent protest, 22
North Carolina Agricultural and Technical College, 24–25

Parks, Rosa, 10, 12, 14, 15, **15, 16,** 17
Pattillo, Melba, 20
Peck, Jim, **26**
"Precious Lord," 11
Project "C," **30,** 31, 32
protest marches, 31, 36, **36,** 44, 45, 46, 47, 48

Ray, Gloria, 20
Roberts, Terrance, 20

segregation, 12, 14, 15, 22, 24, 26, 27, 31, 33
Selma, Alabama, 44, 45
Shores, Arthur, 33
sit-ins, 10, 22, **22–23,** 25, **25,** 31, 35, 36
Southern Christian Leadership Conference (SCLC), 31, 48
Student Nonviolent Coordinating Committee (SNCC), 26, 27
Supreme Court, 17, 18

Thomas, Jefferson, 20

voting rights, 10, 39, 43, 44–45, 46
Voting Rights Act of 1965, 45, 46

Wallace, George, 44
Walls, Carlotta, 20
Washington, D.C., 39, 43
Williams, Hosea, **51**
Women's Political Council, 17
Woolworth store, 24–25, **24**

Young, Andrew, 50

ACKNOWLEDGMENTS

My part in this book is due to many positive forces. I should first thank my mother and father, Earline and Kenneth Duncan, who made it all possible. Many thanks go to librarian Lois Collins for the use of her library collection. And for all of their support and encouragement, I want to thank my "core" group: Shun, Karen, Jeff, and Tim. To the other major players who turned this vision into a reality, I say thanks to Leila Boyd for the morale boost and paper, while much gratitude goes to Jim Smith, Bonnie Brook, Leslie Bauman, and BridgeWater Books for choosing me.

Alice Faye Duncan

I am thankful to many people who helped me with this book—my wife, Anne, who started me on the journey that led to the National Civil Rights Museum, and four wonderful women: Juanita Moore, Leila Boyd, Barbara Andrews, and Rosalyn Nichols, all of whom opened the museum and their hearts to me.

I want to thank my own children, Laura, Luke, and Alison, who were a source of encouragement and humor; and all the children pictured in this book—they were so eager to help!

A special debt of gratitude goes to Matt and Andrew Gillis, Leslie Bauman, Beaura Ringrose, Bonnie Brook, and Alice Faye Duncan, with one final thanks to all the men, women, and children who marched on the journey for civil rights. Their struggle leaves me moved, inspired, and finally humbled.

J. Gerard Smith

CREDITS

Every effort has been made to secure the necessary permissions and make full acknowledgment for their use. If notified of any errors, the publisher will gladly make the necessary corrections in future editions.

Text Credits Excerpts from "Letter from a Birmingham Jail," "I Have a Dream," and "I've Seen the Promised Land," by Dr. Martin Luther King, Jr., reprinted by arrangement with The Heirs to the Estate of Martin Luther King, Jr., c/o Joan Daves Agency as agent for the proprietor. Copyright © 1963 by Martin Luther King, Jr.; copyright renewed 1991 by Coretta Scott King ("Letter from a Birmingham Jail" and "I Have a Dream"). Copyright © 1968 by the Estate of Martin Luther King, Jr. ("I've Seen the Promised Land").

Photo Credits A/P Wide World Photos: 16 (bottom), 20, 21 (right), 24 (photographed by Fred Blackwell), 26 (right), 30 (left), 35, 38, 51; Birmingham News Company: 26 (left); Black Star: 30 (right, photographed by Charles Moore); Life Magazine, Time Warner: 56 (Joseph Law); The National Civil Rights Museum: 16 (top, photographed by Don Craven); UPI/Bettman: 21 (left), 27, 32, 34, 36, 41, 42, 43, 45, 46.

P9-CCR-822

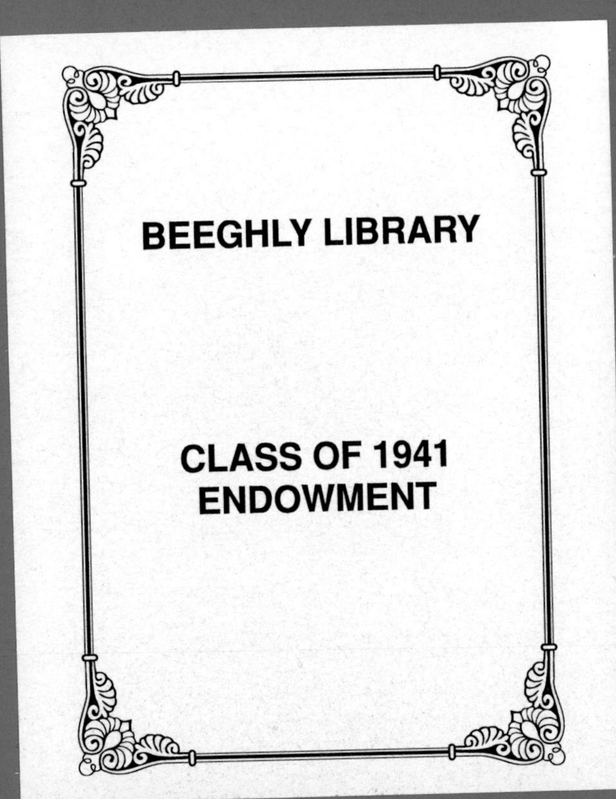
BEEGHLY LIBRARY
CLASS OF 1941
ENDOWMENT

Robert Winston

Evolution Revolution

DK PUBLISHING

LONDON, NEW YORK, MUNICH,
MELBOURNE, and DELHI

Senior editors Deborah Lock, Wendy Horobin
Designers Sadie Thomas, Laura Roberts-Jensen, Claire Patané, Sonia Moore, Vicky Wharton, Clemence de Molliens, Lauren Rosier, Clare Shedden, Tory Gordon-Harris

US editor Margaret Parrish
Picture researcher Myriam Mégharbi
Indexer Chris Bernstein
Production editor Sean Daly
Production controller Clare Pearson
Jacket designers Karen Shooter, Natalie Godwin
Jacket editor Mariza O'Keeffe
Publishing manager Bridget Giles
Art director Rachael Foster
Creative director Jane Bull
Publisher Mary Ling

Consultant Kim Dennis-Bryan
Associate Lecturer of Evolution, Open University

First published in the United States in 2009 by
DK Publishing
375 Hudson Street
New York, New York 10014

09 10 11 12 13 10 9 8 7 6 5 4 3 2
WD186—11/08

A catalog record for this book is available from the Library of Congress.

ISBN: 978-0-7566-4524-3

Color reproduction in UK by Alta Image
Printed and bound by L Rex, China

Discover more at
www.dk.com

"The theory of evolution has been called the greatest scientific idea of all time. In biology—the study of plants and animals—there is no idea that compares with Charles Darwin's thinking about evolution. Although the basic notion that the many species of animals had developed from earlier creatures was not entirely new, Darwin came to riveting conclusions.

He understood that all living things evolved from more primitive forms of life, deciding this process happened over millions of years of tiny changes. Darwin also explained how this was a gradual response to the environment. If a species of animal or plant could not adapt to hostile circumstances, it and its offspring would eventually die out.

Darwin's ideas aroused wonder, criticism, and fury. More than 150 years later, his ideas are still controversial in some parts of the world. It is not easy to accept that we are descended from apes.

Darwin's ideas have become more convincing with time, the more we study biology. Evolution explains how we came to exist, and how we fit into the world around us. Such knowledge helps us understand disease and health, and our emotions and instincts. Above all, the recognition that we are so close to other living organisms gives us greater respect for all life forms on our amazing planet."

Robert Winston.

ROBERT WINSTON

The search for ANSWERS

DARWIN and his theory

All in the GENES

EVOLUTION in action

A book that changed the world 6
The search for answers 8
Creation stories 10
The debate begins 12
Fossil mysteries 14
Revolution! 16

Darwin and his theory 18
A disgrace 20
Big adventure 22
Ups and downs 24
Naturalist at work 26
Select the best 28
The struggle for existence 30
I will survive! 32
Eye wonder 34
Bestseller 36
Post-origin 38

All in the genes 40
The pea plant puzzle 42
Genetic recipe 44
One in a quintillion 46
Mutations 48
We're all mutants 50
Twists of fortune or fate 52
Mystery of mysteries 54
A ghost in your genes 56
For the good of the species? 58
Playing God 60
Jurassic Park 62

Evolution in action 64
Story of life 66
Missing links 72
Islands apart 74
Same, but different 76
Embryos 78
Close relatives 80
Family trees 82
How the elephant got his trunk 84
From ape to human 86
Human behavior 88
Surviving sickness 90
Still evolving 92
Glossary 94

Why is there life on Earth? Where do we come from? For **millennia** people have tried to answer these questions. **In 1858,** *Charles Darwin* unveiled his **theory of natural selection** to explain how **LIFE** evolved on Earth. The following year he finished **ON THE ORIGIN OF SPECIES, a book that changed the world**. It challenged the status of *humans* and sparked debates about the development of *species* that continue *today*.

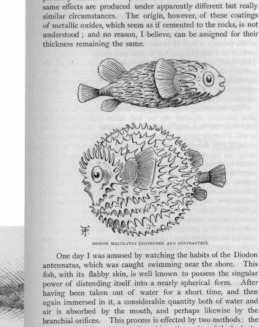

I *HABITS OF A DIODON* 13

the limits of the tidal waves; and as the rivulet slowly trickles down, the surf must supply the polishing power of the cataracts in the great rivers. In like manner, the rise and fall of the tide probably answer to the periodical inundations; and thus the same effects are produced under apparently different but really similar circumstances. The origin, however, of these coatings of metallic oxides, which seem as if cemented to the rocks, is not understood; and no reason, I believe, can be assigned for their thickness remaining the same.

DIODON MACULATUS (DISTENDED AND CONTRACTED).

One day I was amused by watching the habits of the Diodon antennatus, which was caught swimming near the shore. This fish, with its flabby skin, is well known to possess the singular power of distending itself into a nearly spherical form. After having been taken out of water for a short time, and then again immersed in it, a considerable quantity both of water and air is absorbed by the mouth, and perhaps likewise by the branchial orifices. This process is effected by two methods: the air is swallowed, and is then forced into the cavity of the body, its

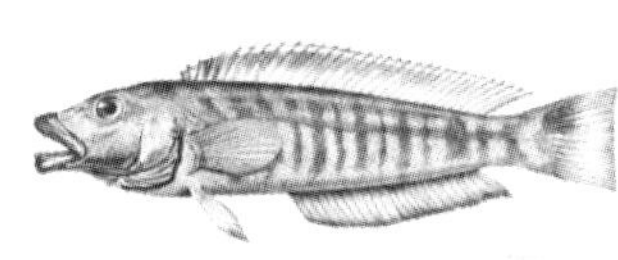

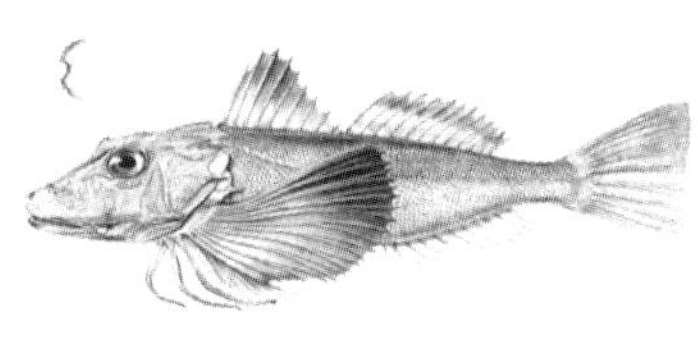

"*Whilst this planet has gone cycling on according to* fixed laws of gravity, *from so* **SIMPLE** *a beginning... endless forms most beautiful and most wonderful, have been, and are being* **evolved**."

—Charles Darwin (1858)

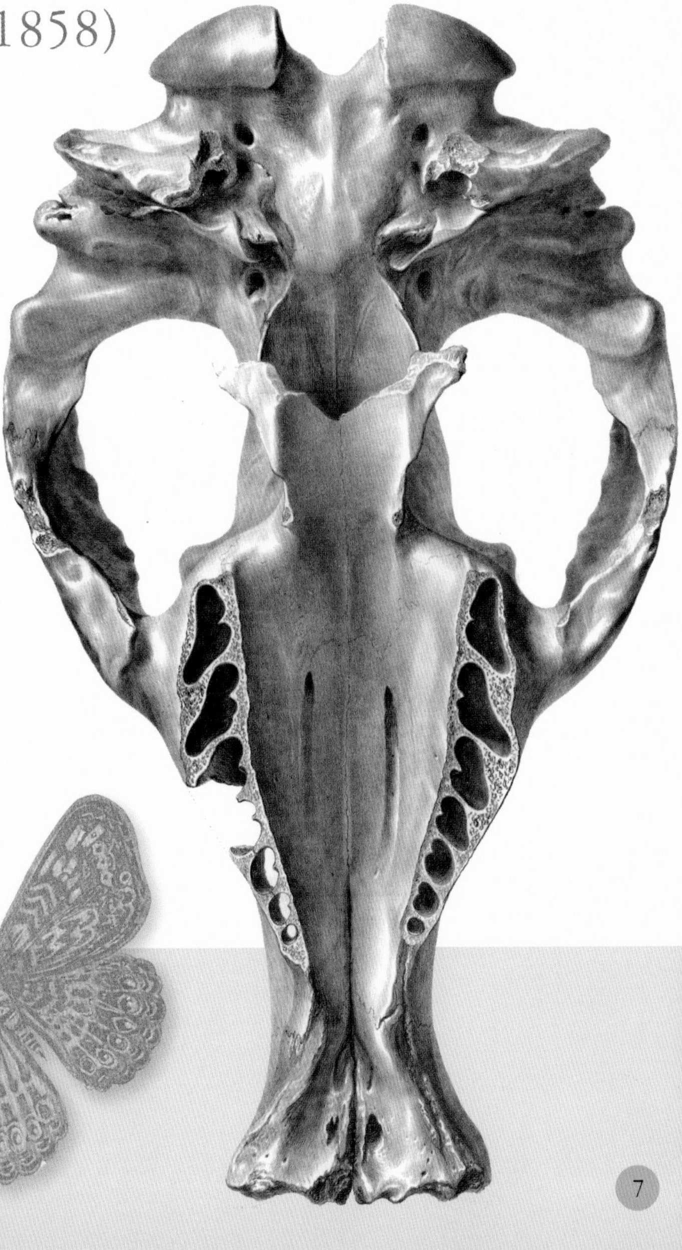

"The *war of nature is not incessant,* **death** *is generally prompt, and the vigorous, the healthy, and the happy* **survive** *and* **multiply.**"

—Charles Darwin (1859)

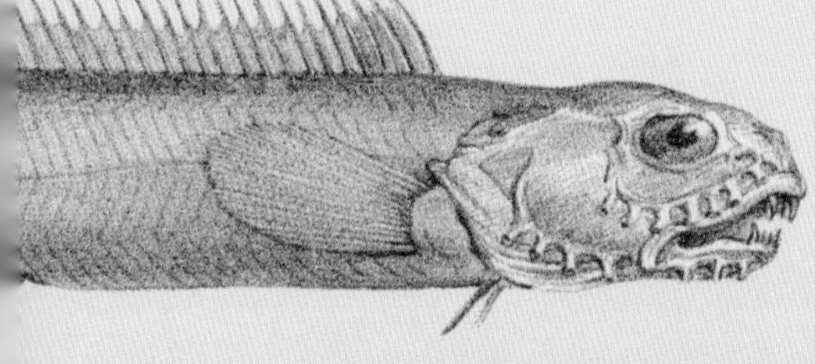

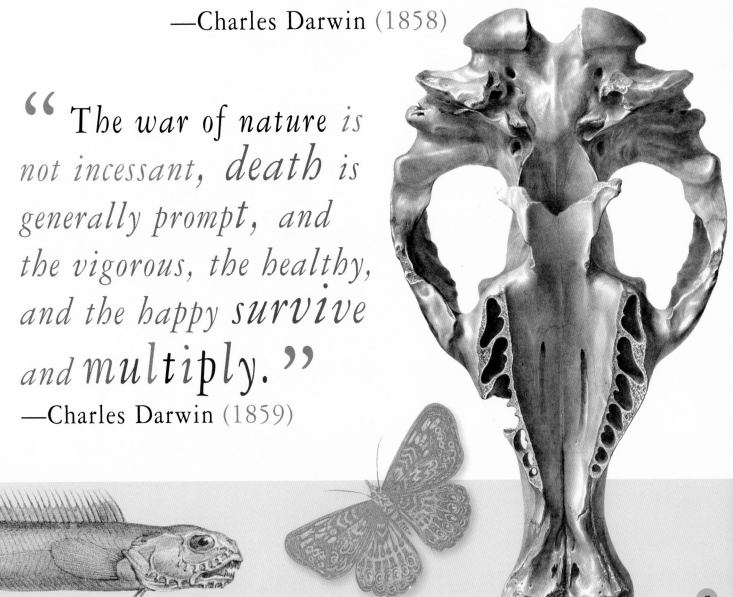

People say we're descended from dinosaurs! *That's why we have scaly legs.*

We long-necked types *must surely* be higher up the evolutionary ladder.

Apparently, some people think that *evolution* is a load of old bull!

THE SEARCH FOR ANSWERS

Have you ever stopped and taken a moment to watch an insect, peer into a flower, or listen to the birds?

How come everything seems to be so perfectly adapted to its environment?

Have you ever marveled at how many different types, or species, of creatures and plants there are?

You are not the first to ponder over these observations. People have been wondering and questioning for many hundreds of years. And trying to answer the biggest mystery of all: how were we all made?

Hey, salamander, I hear you were once hot stuff!

Yep, those medieval folk thought I was *"created"* in the *flames of a fire.*

Creation stories

In the flickering light of a campfire, people living long ago tried to explain how animals, plants, and people were created. Around the world, their stories varied, telling of one God or many gods or spirits creating life, and these tales were passed down from generation to generation.

GREEK MYTHS

According to an ancient Greek story, the laurel tree was formed when Daphne, a river nymph who was being chased by the god of love, Apollo, cried out in exhaustion to Gaia, the Mother Earth god. Gaia turned Daphne into the tree.

Daphne becomes a laurel tree.

Job's done! Time to go back to sleep.

DREAMTIME

Aborigines believe that all forms of life, the Ancestors, lay sleeping underneath the crust of Earth. Awoken when time split apart, they wandered around the Earth calling all living things into being and showing them how to live.

In the beginning...

I need some excitement around here.

BRAHMA

The Hindu god of creation, Brahma, used the lotus flower he had been sitting on in a vast dark ocean to create the world and all living things. To the plants he gave feeling and to all animals he gave the senses of touch and smell and the power to see, hear, and move.

Lotus flower

PACIFIC TALES

The early people living on some islands in the Pacific Ocean told stories of the first people hatching from eggs laid by a bird-headed god or turtle.

The Garden of Eden

Genesis, the first book of the Bible, tells of everything being created by God in six days. Each species of animal was independently created, perfectly designed for a specific purpose. Adam and Eve were made in God's likeness, so they were different from animals and given a more important role. In Western Europe, the deep-rooted religious belief in this story influenced scientific thinking for many years.

Skunk

Sacred spirits

A Native American tale tells of a beautiful but vain white-haired girl who one day rudely mocked a strange-looking man. The man revealed himself to be one of the great spirits. In anger, the spirit turned the girl into a skunk. Her beautiful hair became the furry white stripe down her back. She was the first of the species of skunk.

James Ussher (1581–1656)

Creation day

After carefully calculating the ages of people mentioned in the Bible, James Ussher, an Irish Archbishop, believed he knew the exact date of the biblical Creation—Sunday, October 23, 4004 BCE. This made Earth less than 6,000 years old.

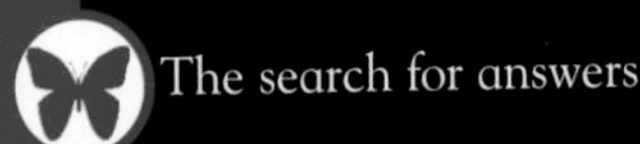

The *debate* begins...

Order! Order! Everything needs to be in order.

The birth of the classification system

The botanist Carl Linnaeus grouped all known living things into categories, arranging them into a "Divine Order of God's creation." He devised a system that divided living things into kingdoms, classes, orders, genera, and species. He gave each plant and animal two Latin names made up of the genus (or group) and the species, which scientists still use today. He classified humans as *Homo sapiens* meaning "wise man."

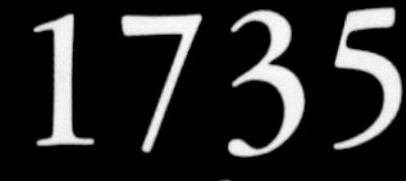
Carl Linnaeus (1707–1778)

I abandon everything in my book.
Sniff, sniff!

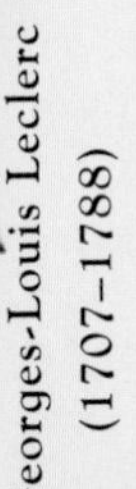
Georges-Louis Leclerc (1707–1788)

1735 **1749**

Species *Homo sapiens*

Genus *Homo*

Family Hominidae

Order Primates

Class Mammalia

Kingdom Animalia

Linnaeus has grouped us with apes!
Was that God's intention?

Buffon's Laws of Nature

The Comte de Buffon, Georges-Louis Leclerc, wrote a 44-volume natural history book series between 1749 and 1804, but only published a few copies. He put forward the idea that all living things had been modified from a single ancestor through natural laws working in the environment or by chance. **Shock, horror!** ***He was challenging the biblical Genesis story.*** Without proof though, he was unable to justify his views, which were seen as against God. He was later forced to issue a public withdrawal of them.

Botanists and naturalists throughout the 18th century *classified and observed plants and studied vertebrate and invertebrate animals.* Some scientists began to *question and challenge* the popular belief that God had created all species as they appear now. Murmurings about species having evolved began to stir up a heated debate.

A pupil of Buffon, *Chevalier de Lamarck* was the first to confidently and very publicly publish a theory of evolution. *He suggested that living things changed by a process of two forces pulling against each other.*

Lamarck suggested that the changes involved in both forces were due to SUBTLE FLUIDS. These flowed all around the body, producing movement and change. For example, snails have poor sight and Lamarck imagined an ancestral snail with no feelers trying to feel its way around. In doing so, "masses of nervous fluid as well as other liquids" would be sent to the front of the head, which in time would produce extended feelers.

Feelers at last!

Chevalier de Lamarck (1744–1829)

1809 But Lamarck's thinking could be easily attacked and discredited by critics.

If he were correct about inheriting acquired features then the children of professional weightlifters would be born with bulging muscles.

Lamarck's changing forces

Force 1 All living things began as simple organisms and then progressed by changing gradually to become more complex and perfect. Lamarck thought humans had reached perfection. He also suggested that the simple organisms were created continuously by "spontaneous generation" from nonliving matter, such as wet straw. (Later, the French microbiologist, Louis Pasteur, boiled some straw but nothing developed.)

Force 2 Animals underwent a bodily change during their lifetimes to fit into their environment. These favorable changes were then passed on to their offspring. Changes would be made either by the use or the disuse of a feature. For example, a giraffe's neck would become longer by stretching farther to get the leaves in the trees.

Fossil *mysteries*

Since ancient times, the finding of fossils has fascinated people. To begin with, people wondered what they were and did they have magical powers. Once people realized that fossils came from dead creatures, questions arose about why so many fossils of sea creatures were found on mountaintops. After finding an answer to this that fit with the Bible, a further discovery of giant fossils made everyone have to think again.

After the flood, we all had lots of babies.

According to the Bible story, Noah took every animal species on board his ark during the Great Flood.

Diluvialism theory

Up until the end of the 18th century, diluvialism was a popular theory. The theory goes that Earth's surface was reshaped during the great biblical flood when it rained for 40 days and 40 nights. All fossils were drowned creatures that had been formed at this time. The high waters had carried sea creatures to mountaintops and left them there as the waters went down.

1817

Fossilized teeth of a mosasaur

Fossils of giants

During the 1700s, fossils of giant creatures were being discovered and described, including the mosasaur, a giant marine reptile. People believed that the creatures must still exist since Noah had saved them. But where were they now? They would be so large that even in unexplored areas, these gigantic creatures would be unable to hide themselves.

Extinction idea

After studying fossils found in the area around Paris, the naturalist Georges Cuvier concluded that they were thousands of centuries old. His observations increased the age of Earth well beyond the accepted 6,000 years. Cuvier also noted that these fossils did not look like anything still living, so these creatures must now be ***extinct***.

Georges Cuvier (1769–1832)

Catastrophe theory

Much admired for his brilliant mind, Georges Cuvier concluded from his fossil and natural history studies that Earth had been dramatically reshaped by a series of ***major catastrophes***—the last one being the biblical flood. In his opinion, other floods, earthquakes, and climate changes had caused the previous catastrophes.

Cuvier's wrong and I'm right! The watermarks on these ruined pillars prove that in the last 2,000 years, the land has dropped below sea level and then slowly been pushed up again.

Rock of ages

Fascinated by rocks, the geologist Charles Lyell had a totally opposing view to Cuvier's catastrophe theory. He proposed that the reshaping of Earth in the past had been formed by the same ***gradual changes*** as can be seen now. For the first page of his book *The Principles of Geology*, Lyell chose an engraving of the ancient temple of Serapis.

Charles Lyell (1797–1875)

The ancient temple of Serapis.

1830 1831

Rebuilding giants

At the Natural History Museum in Paris, Cuvier became famous for being able to construct a complete animal from just a few fossil bones. One of his most famous reconstructions was the giant elephantlike creature called the mastodon. Cuvier was surprisingly accurate.

Trip of a lifetime

In 1831, a young naturalist, Charles Darwin, joined a survey ship HMS *Beagle* on a five-year voyage around the world. He took with him Lyell's book and, throughout the voyage, he saw rock formations and experienced earthquakes that convinced him Lyell was right about the land slowly reshaping.

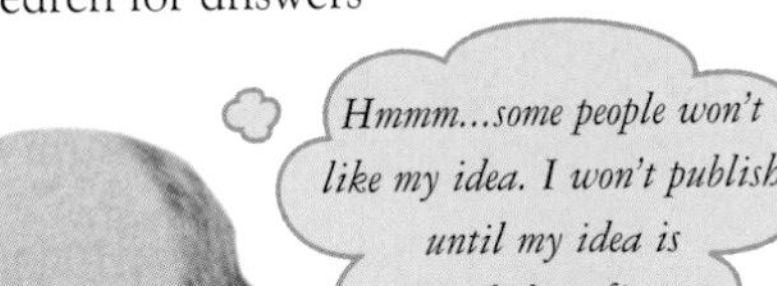
Hmmm...some people won't like my idea. I won't publish until my idea is foolproof!

Revolution!

Darwin's idea of *evolution* slowly dawned on him after returning from his voyage. But he knew from *Lamarck's* and others' experiences that he would not be taken seriously without sound evidence. So he set about researching. It was a further *20 years* before Darwin announced his **THEORY OF NATURAL SELECTION,** which would send shockwaves across the scientific community.

Darwin's big idea

To work, natural selection needs three things:

1 Variation

All individuals within a species have different characteristics, or ***variations***. More individuals are born than will survive to adulthood.

WE'RE ALL SLIGHTLY DIFFERENT, BUT I HAVE THE **BIGGEST** EARS AND THE **THICKEST** FUR. SO I CAN HEAR AND STAY WARM THE BEST.

1859

1860

Published

On the Origin of Species, published in 1859, was an "abstract," or summary, of Darwin's theory of how living things had evolved, which he proposed was through a process he called "***natural selection.***" He intended to write a more detailed book later but never did.

Outrage!

Seven months later, the British Association held a meeting of well-respected scientists and philosphers inside the Oxford University Museum to debate whether natural things had evolved. Most vocal for the *"Yes, they did!"* view was the biologist, Thomas Huxley, and for the *"No, they didn't!"* view was Bishop Samuel Wilberforce. The meeting ended in uproar.

WILBERFORCE
HUXLEY

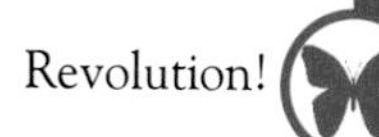

The greyhound has been bred to have great eyesight and amazing running speed.

Artificial selection

Darwin learned much from breeders of plants and animals, who saw the small variations between individuals. A dog breeder would choose a desired feature and mate two dogs with that feature. The puppies with this chosen feature would be picked out and bred. Over many generations, the feature would become more obvious. Darwin realized a similar process was happening in the wild.

2 Competition

With so many individuals competing against each other, the slight variations among them give some a better chance of survival than others in their environment.

Who Survives? *Nature* Decides!

3 Inheritance

Because they are more successful, some variations occur more often than others. Over many generations, a noticeable modification, or adaptation, might be seen. Over time, these changes could result in a ***new species.***

Darwin published more books.

1871

Darwin continued to publish books, applying his thinking about how natural selection worked. In **The Descent of Man,** Darwin argued that humans shared a common ancestor with apes.

1872

Darwin sparked scientists' interest in animal behavior when he stated that there were links between the way animals and humans expressed emotion in **The Expression of the Emotions in Man and Animals.**

1880

In **The Power of Movement in Plants,** Darwin explained how climbing plants had evolved their ability to grow upward to get more sunlight.

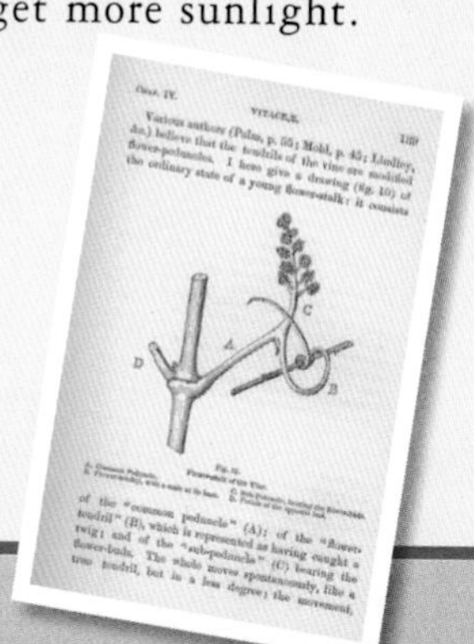

What's taking you so long?

DARWIN AND HIS THEORY

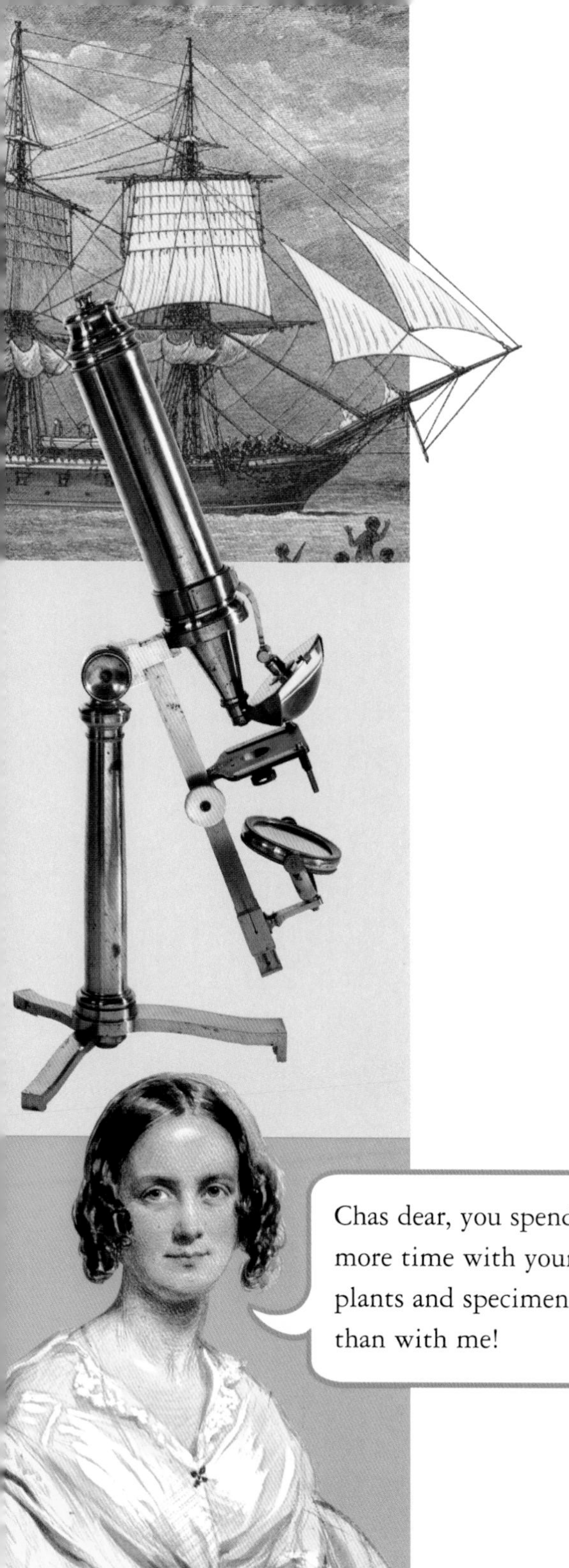

Chas dear, you spend more time with your plants and specimens than with me!

Can you imagine yourself working in secret on a brilliant idea you've had for over 20 years, not letting anyone know except a couple of close friends? That's just what Charles Darwin did, and the hard work was worth it!

When he eventually published his theory of natural selection, supported by a hefty load of evidence, Darwin became internationally famous.

Even 150 years later his work is still being mentioned in books like this one.

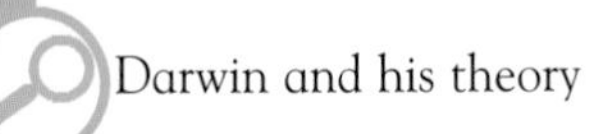

A *disgrace*

Darwin's family wanted Charles to be a doctor, but he had other interests. A "classics" schooling bored him, while collecting natural objects fascinated him. A "gory" doctor's training disgusted him, while hunting and expeditions into the countryside thrilled him. Was Charles going to become an "idle sporting man" as his father feared or would he make his mark on the world as was expected of a Darwin?

LOOK WHAT I'VE FOUND!

Darwin aged 7

FAMILY CONNECTIONS

Darwin was born into a large, successful, and well-to-do family. His mother was a daughter of Josiah Wedgwood, who had established a successful pottery business. His other grandfather was Erasmus Darwin, who was a highly respected physician and biologist. His large and imposing father, Robert Darwin, was also a physician.

CUP OF TEA?

Josiah Wedgwood

Erasmus Darwin

The Mount—Darwin's family home

Wedgwood cup

In 1794, Erasmus had published an influential scientific book, *Zoonomia*, written in rhyming couplets, that had included his thoughts about evolution.

"You care for NOTHING but *shooting* dogs, and *rat catching*, and you *will*

Student days

Charles was sent first to the University of Edinburgh, Scotland, at age 16 to become a doctor but he felt too squeamish to perform operations. When this option failed, he went to the University of Cambridge, England, to study to become a clergyman. However, he was not interested in studying these subjects and much preferred to meet up with friends interested in animals and plants.

A zoology lecturer at Edinburgh, Dr. Robert Grant, shared an interest in sea creatures with Darwin, and together they collected animals in tidal pools. Darwin had an even greater friendship with John Henslow, a professor of botany at Cambridge who had expert knowledge about plants, insects, chemistry, minerals, and rock formations. He often joined Henslow on trips into the countryside, finding out about rare plants and animals.

Charles helped his older brother, Erasmus, to do chemistry experiments in the homemade laboratory set up in a tool shed in their yard. Often they stayed up late together, making gases and chemical mixtures. Charles' school friends found out and gave him the nickname "Gas." The headmaster, who considered the classics—Latin and Greek—more important than science, once publicly berated Darwin for wasting his time on this useless subject.

Charles's great joy was hunting—shooting birds, rabbits, and foxes. He would visit Maer, his uncle's estate, or Woodhouse, the home of a family friend. Charles would place his shooting boots ready beside his bed so he would waste no time in getting into them first thing in the morning. He kept a record of how many birds he had shot by tying knots in a piece of string attached to a buttonhole.

be a DISGRACE to *yourself* and ALL your *family*." ROBERT DARWIN, *his father*

Big *adventure*

After graduating college, Darwin returned home uncertain of his future. Awaiting him there was a letter that would change his life. It was from John Henslow, who had turned down an opportunity to be the naturalist on board the survey ship HMS *Beagle*, which was to sail around the world. He had recommended that Darwin should go in his place.

The Captain, ***Robert FitzRoy***, nearly prevented Darwin from joining the voyage because he didn't like the shape of his nose!

The HMS *Beagle* set out with a crew of 73 men.

Around the world

The HMS *Beagle* set sail from England in December 1831 and finally returned home five years later in October 1836.

Darwin's telescope

GENERAL CHART shewing the PRINCIPAL TRACKS of H.M.S. BEAGLE _ 1831-6.

1835

1832

1833-1834

1836

1836

Start voyage: England 1831

End voyage: England 1836

= Journey to Galápagos

= Journey back to England

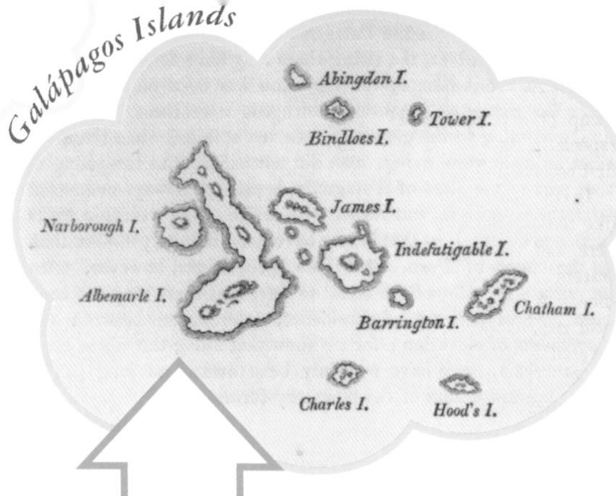

Curious isles

After nearly four years surveying the coastline of South America, the HMS *Beagle* sailed to the nearby cluster of black-lava rock islands of the Galápagos. On his island excursions, Darwin collected many rocks and plants and used his hunting skills to capture animals, particularly birds, to take back to England.

Darwin saw the world's largest variety of tortoise on the Galápagos. Local people told him that they knew which island a tortoise had come from just by looking at its shell.

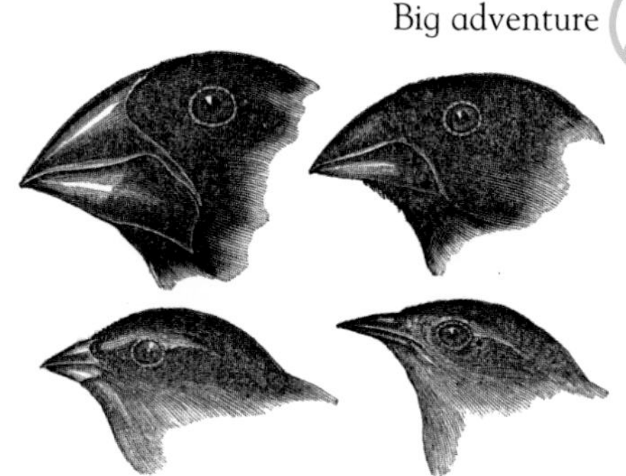

Beak mystery

Darwin was fascinated by the different beak shapes of the birds he saw. He did not realize until after he had returned home that the 13 species he collected were all finches. He would later conclude that the finches had evolved from a shared ancestor and each species had developed a different beak to adapt to eating different foods for survival.

Marine iguana

The "swarms" of marine iguanas lying on the rocks horrified the crew. They are the only iguanas that swim in the sea to feed. They return to the rocks to warm up.

Making waves

In August 1839, Darwin published his diary of the *Beagle* voyage. This book summarized his findings and insights about the local and colonial people he met. It was well received and he established himself as a popular author.

Weird and wonderful

Darwin collected thousands of specimens during the voyage. He and his assistant, Syms Covington, kept them from decaying by either removing their innards and stuffing them with cotton, or placing them in jars of wine and sealing tightly. Once home, he sent many of the specimens to various botanists and naturalists, who made detailed drawings of them.

Darwin's scorpion fish drawn by Leonard Jenyns, naturalist

A parrotfish caught by Darwin and preserved in wine.

JOURNAL OF RESEARCHES
INTO THE
NATURAL HISTORY & GEOLOGY
OF THE
COUNTRIES VISITED DURING THE VOYAGE ROUND THE WORLD OF H.M.S. 'BEAGLE'
UNDER THE COMMAND OF CAPTAIN FITZ ROY, R.N.

BY CHARLES DARWIN, M.A., F.R.S.

A NEW EDITION
WITH ILLUSTRATIONS BY R. T. PRITCHETT OF PLACES VISITED AND OBJECTS DESCRIBED

LONDON
JOHN MURRAY, ALBEMARLE STREET
1890

UPS and *downs*

Hurray! Darwin's finally home.
Loved your letters! More! More!

On his return to England, Darwin found himself already a scientific *celebrity*. Henslow had distributed a few of Darwin's letters from his voyage among scientists, who had been IMPRESSED. Enthusiastically, Darwin started the huge task of organizing his notes and cataloging all the specimens he had collected, but a mysterious illness was to slow him down.

Puzzling illness

Shortly after returning from his voyage, Darwin began to suffer from violent sickness, severe pain, and dizziness. Doctors, including his father, were unable to identify the cause and could not suggest a cure. Had he been bitten by some strange creature while on his voyage? This mysterious illness occurred frequently throughout the rest of his life, which meant that Darwin was forced to stay at home.

DOWN HOUSE

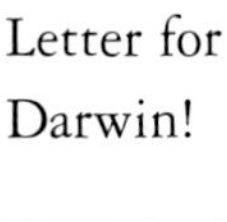
Letter for Darwin!

Married life

After making a list of the advantages and disadvantages of marrying, Darwin concluded that this would be a good idea. He married his cousin, Emma Wedgwood. She was nicknamed "little Miss Slip-Slop" because of her messiness, but that didn't bother Darwin. Just before the birth of their third child, the family moved from London to a large house and grounds, called Down House, in easy reach of London. Here, Darwin lived happily with Emma and his 10 children.

*"Write a letter, write a letter,
Good advice will make us better."*

A man of letters

Stuck at home, Darwin kept in touch with people through letters. Darwin corresponded with over 2,000 people during his lifetime. They were not just scientists, but also gardeners, gamekeepers, animal and plant breeders, and those traveling or located abroad. Darwin received over 14,000 letters and probably wrote more than 7,000.

Secret notebooks

In July 1837, Darwin had the beginnings of an idea that he knew would spark a **HUGE** debate about the *religious thinking* of the time. He began *scribbling* his thoughts into the first of many notebooks, which he would ***keep secret***.

He sketched a branching tree to show a family history for animals where they shared a common ancestor. He believed that species had changed over time. But what process had made this happen? Darwin knew his idea had to be supported and set about gathering evidence and experimenting.

A bat's wing is supported by elongated finger bones.

Bones in common

All mammals share the same basic patterns of limb bones. These similarities suggest that they share a common ancestor.

WOLF PAW

PORPOISE FLIPPER

BAT WING

Darwin only shared his thoughts on evolution with two of his closest friends. Charles Lyell was an expert on rock formations and Joseph Hooker was an expert on plants.

Naturalist at work

Darwin's microscope

Every day, Darwin spent many hours in his study or his garden experimenting, observing, and analyzing plants, animals, and rocks. He filled his secret notebooks with any evidence of species evolving. In 1844, he wrote a 189-page manuscript outlining his evolutionary theory, but he still didn't publish and continued to collect evidence.

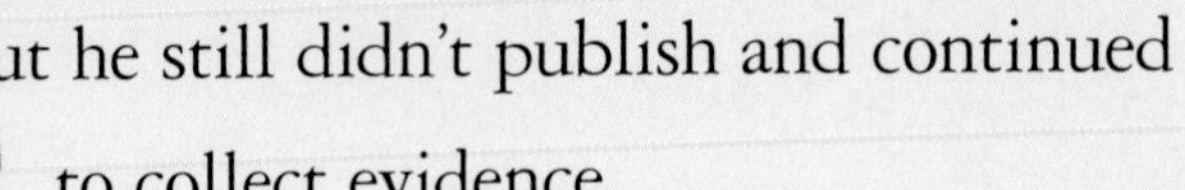

A drawer containing some of Darwin's specimens

Darwin collected 1,529 species

Kitchen garden

The garden of Down House became a laboratory—a place for investigating and experimenting. Within the large walled vegetable and flower garden, Darwin built his greenhouse, where he set up many experiments to understand the pollination, fertilization, and adaptability of plants.

Buzz!
I like that bee over there. I've been fooled—
it's only an orchid!

Daily routine: Walk before breakfast; 8:00 Work in study; 9:30 Read letters; 10:30 Work; 12:00 Walk;

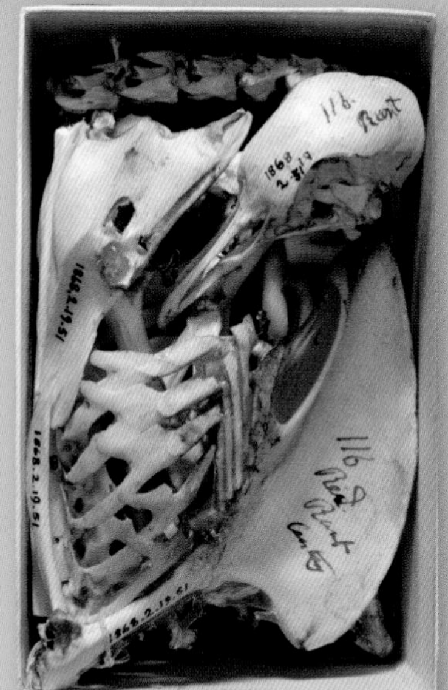

Fancy pigeons

Darwin bought many breeds of domestic pigeon and became convinced through analyzing their features that they were all descended from the rock dove. The pigeons showed him how much variation in color, shape, feathers, and bone structure existed in a single type of animal.

The skeleton of a pigeon, bred, examined, and labeled by Darwin as part of his research on evolution.

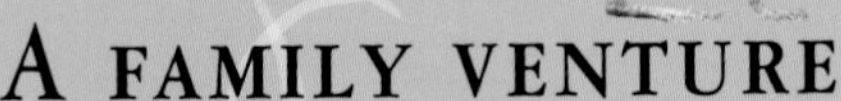

Skeleton of a mouse

A family venture

On occasions, members of the household were involved in collecting information for Darwin. His children tracked the flight patterns of bumblebees and noted the locations of spider webs. Even their governess joined them in counting plant species in a meadow. Servants would help him boil carcasses of small mice and birds so that their skeletons could be studied.

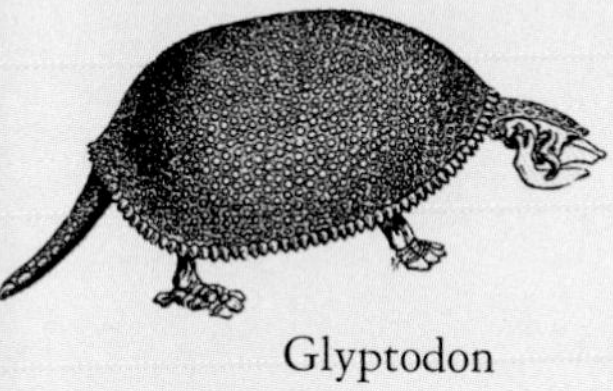
Glyptodon

Fossil findings

In South America, Darwin found remains of a giant armored animal, a glyptodon, which he realized looked similar to the smaller armadillos he saw. Was this evidence of a species that had evolved?

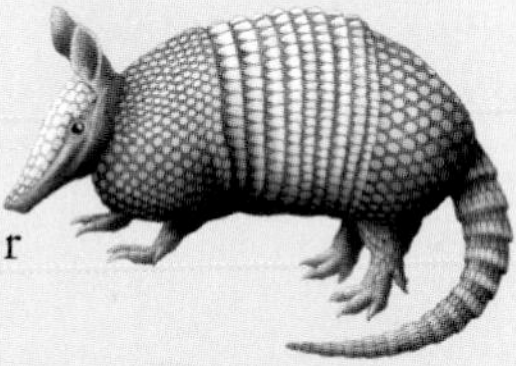
Armadillo

Under the microscope

Darwin wanted to establish himself as an expert on one particular species and chose the subject of barnacles.

Barnacles

Darwin became fascinated with them and became deeply involved in the subject for eight years. He was sent a huge number of barnacles and fossils of barnacles and was able to see how there were many species and that they were all related to each other.

Darwin's rhea

Darwin came across a rare species of rhea in part of South America. This was different from the more common rhea in that area. Did the two species have a common ancestor?

Darwin's rhea

and 3,907 other specimens on his voyage.

Greenhouse lab

Darwin was fascinated by the shape of an orchid and after numerous tests he was convinced that these flowers and the insects that pollinated them had evolved together to become perfectly adapted.

The lower petals of the bee orchid have evolved to look like a bee, fooling male bees into visiting and pollinating the flower.

1:00 Lunch; 1:30 Work; 3:00 Rest; 4:00 Walk; 4:30 Work; 5:30 Rest; 7:30 Supper; 8:00 Family games; 10:30 Bed.

Now try this!

Make a collection box using a shoebox, some little boxes, cardboard, and a shoelace.

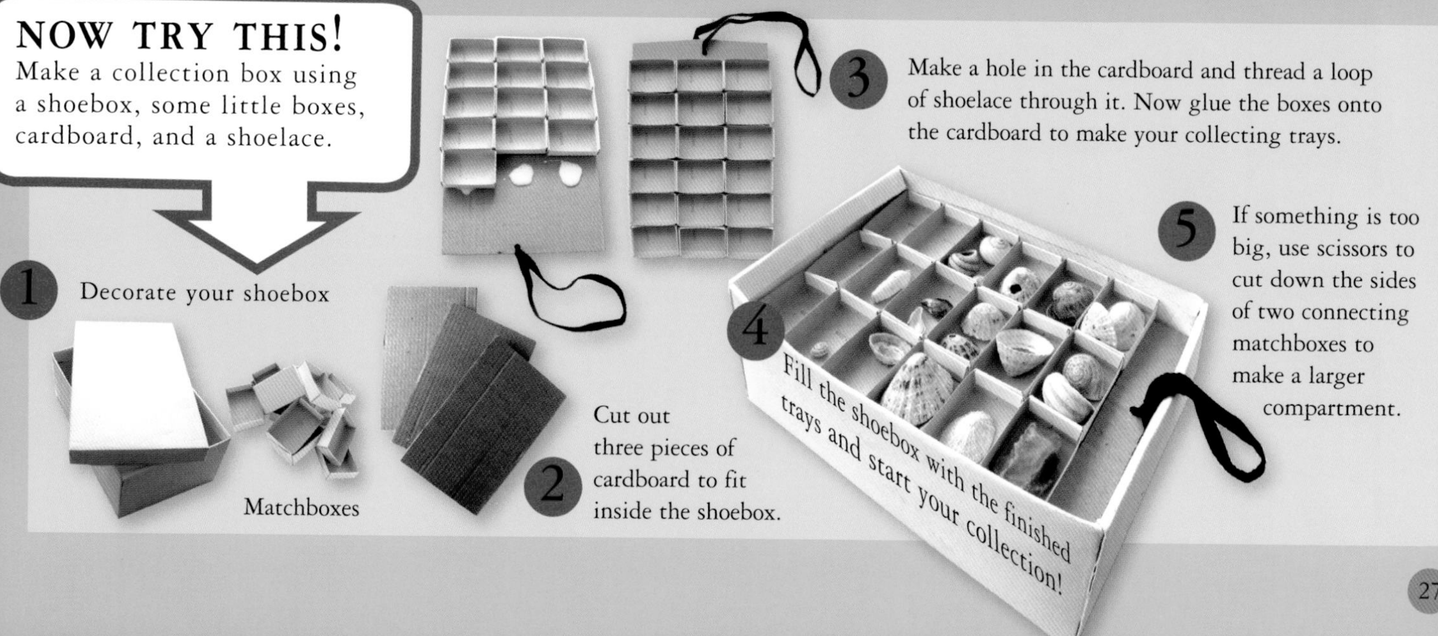

1 Decorate your shoebox

Matchboxes

2 Cut out three pieces of cardboard to fit inside the shoebox.

3 Make a hole in the cardboard and thread a loop of shoelace through it. Now glue the boxes onto the cardboard to make your collecting trays.

4 Fill the shoebox with the finished trays and start your collection!

5 If something is too big, use scissors to cut down the sides of two connecting matchboxes to make a larger compartment.

SELECT THE BEST

Darwin's theory that species in the wild had evolved through a process of **NATURAL SELECTION** had its roots in understanding that for many thousands of years, *people had been very **selective in developing plants** by collecting seeds only from those* **PLANTS WITH THE PREFERRED FEATURE**. The great variety of different-looking vegetables within the cabbage family was an obvious example to Darwin.

Leafy buds

In Belgium, growers were selecting cabbages with tightly packed leafy buds along the main stem. Over time, the plants began producing more and more of these buds and **BY THE 18TH CENTURY** Brussels sprouts had been developed.

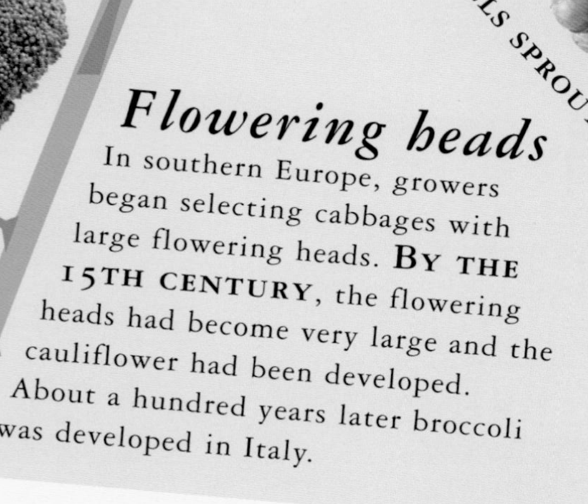

Flowering heads

In southern Europe, growers began selecting cabbages with large flowering heads. **BY THE 15TH CENTURY**, the flowering heads had become very large and the cauliflower had been developed. About a hundred years later broccoli was developed in Italy.

Tight clusters + flowering head = Cauliflower and broccoli

Large leaves + tight clusters = Cabbage

Tight clusters

A large cluster of tightly packed leaves called the cabbage "head" was developed by some people who began selecting seeds from kale plants with a tight cluster of leaves in the center at the top of the stem. Over hundreds of successive generations, plants formed with tighter and larger cluster of leaves taking over the whole plant. This progress was completed in the **1ST CENTURY**.

KOHLRABI

FAT STEM

Over the next 500 years, people were selecting kale plants with short fleshy stems. This selective process produced plants with fatter and fatter stems, which we call kohlrabi. Today, kohlrabi may have white, green, or purple stems.

Large leaves + fat stems = Kohlrabi

KALE

Large leaves

By the **5TH CENTURY BCE**, a large crinkled-leaf plant had been developed, which we call kale. This is one of the oldest crops and is still grown today.

LEAFY VEGETABLE

The wild cabbage is a type of mustard plant that grows naturally around the Mediterranean Sea in Europe. **ANCIENT PEOPLE** collected its seeds and began growing it as a leafy vegetable. **SEEDS FROM THE PLANTS WITH THE LARGEST LEAVES WERE SELECTED FOR THE NEXT YEAR'S CROP.** Larger and larger-leafed plants were slowly being developed.

WILD CABBAGE

In the beginning...

Through a process of ***artificial selection*** the cabbage family is very WIDE and *varied*.

RED CABBAGE

BOK CHOI

By controlling the *pollination process*, growers can combine different cabbage plants and create new strange-looking varieties known as **HYBRIDS**. This process is called **cross-pollination.**

+ =

BROCCOFLOWER

The struggle for existence

Many animals lay hundreds of eggs each year but few develop, hatch, and reach adulthood. Darwin recognized this, but it took him years to realize that this loss of life could be the driving force behind **evolution.**

Nine years before Darwin published *On the Origin of Species*, the poet Alfred Lord Tennyson wrote his poem *In Memoriam* (1850). It contained the phrase that came to represent people's hatred for Darwin's idea of natural selection in the 1800s:

"Nature, red in tooth and claw..."

In 1798, the Reverend Thomas Malthus published *An Essay on the Principle of Population,* which argued that, in the case of humans, numbers are only controlled by famine and disease. His essay was to inspire Darwin's ideas about evolution.

I'M NOT AMUSED! IT'S 1838—FORTY YEARS HAVE GONE BY AND DARWIN IS **ONLY JUST** GETTING AROUND TO READING MY ESSAY. TYPICAL!

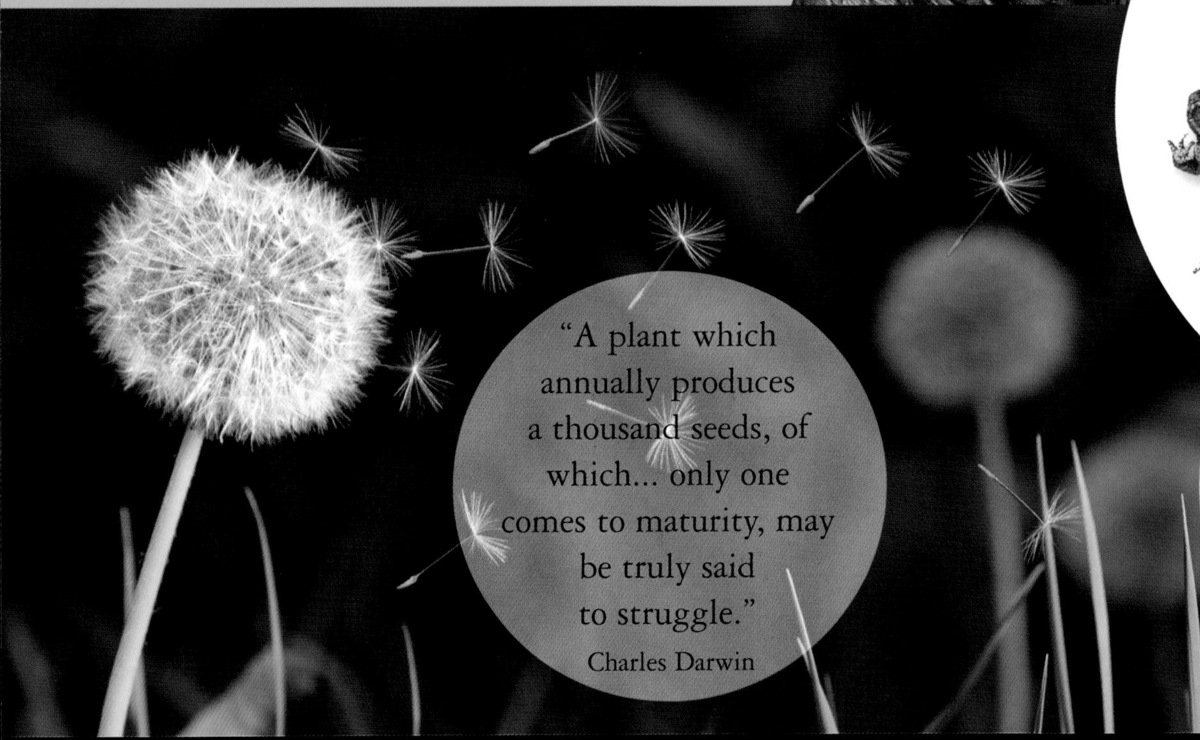

"A plant which annually produces a thousand seeds, of which... only one comes to maturity, may be truly said to struggle."
Charles Darwin

If all the froglets survived, the world would be knee-deep in frogs *within 10 years.*

The numbers game

Out of **hundreds** of froglets:

- **Most** are eaten by predators;
- **Many** die from sickness;
- **Some** die from starvation;
- **Only** one or two live long enough to breed.

Frogs have hundreds of babies but only a few *survive!*

I *will* SURVIVE!

Darwin *recognized* that the individuals that SURVIVE and go on to reproduce tended to be the ones with a *competitive edge* over their rivals. These individuals were *"naturally selected"* to have offspring, which would be more likely to inherit the useful feature.

WINNING *characteristics* in nature:

Impressive feathers

The male peacock's tail seems clumsy, but to a female peacock looking for a mate, the males with the most "eyes" on their tails have an advantage. These individuals have been sexually selected. They would attract more females and have more offspring than plainer peacocks. Over time the feathers have become even more elaborate.

Tough antlers

Stags fight their rivals and the strongest ones with the largest antlers go on to mate and pass on their strength and the size of their antlers to their offspring. Over time the males have become much bigger than the females and have developed very large antlers as a result of sexual selection.

Well hidden

Red grouse are found in heather and black grouse are found in peaty areas. Their colorings keep them well camouflaged, protecting the grouse from predators. If black grouse had lived in heather, they would have been quickly spotted by predators and would not have survived to breed. The red grouse became more and more common in this environment.

Cross-fertilization

Flowering plants have ***evolved to cross-fertilize*** since these individuals can OUT-COMPETE the species that ***self-fertilize***. Many of the bright flowers we see today have adapted to make sure they will be ***cross-fertilized*** to produce lots of healthy offspring.

Best adapted

For natural selection to work, there needs to be an existing feature that can be modified and improved upon. Darwin tested **insect-eating plants** called *sundews* to find out how they knew when to trap an insect but not be sensitive to a nonliving object, such as a *feather*. Then he fed some with small pieces of MEAT and these grew ***quicker*** and produced **MORE** flowers than those that were not fed. He concluded that being able to trap and digest insects was a *favorable characteristic*. **Breakthrough!**

I'm starving!

Now try this!

Try one of Darwin's experiments: In the following test he showed that plant species had a selective advantage if they cross-pollinated with other individuals rather than self-pollinated. Darwin used common toadflax but any plant that produces seeds in a pod will do.

1. Grow six plants. Cover three of the plants with fine netting to prevent insects from getting to their flowers.

2. Wait until the pods form. Select the five best pods from each of the covered and uncovered groups.

3. Count the seeds in each pod and record the number for the covered and uncovered groups. What do you notice? You should find that the number of seeds is greater in the pods of the uncovered plants.

4. Now plant 10 seeds from the uncovered group and 10 seeds from the covered group into pots. Label the groups. Keep all the seedlings warm and watered.

5. Measure the height of the young plants. What do you notice? You should find that the plants whose seeds came from the covered group are shorter than the plants whose seeds came from the uncovered group.

Explanation:

Insects carrying pollen from plant to plant had visited the uncovered plants and so these had been cross-fertilized to produce plants with good growth. The covered plants had not been visited by insects so had self-fertilized, producing plants with poor growth.

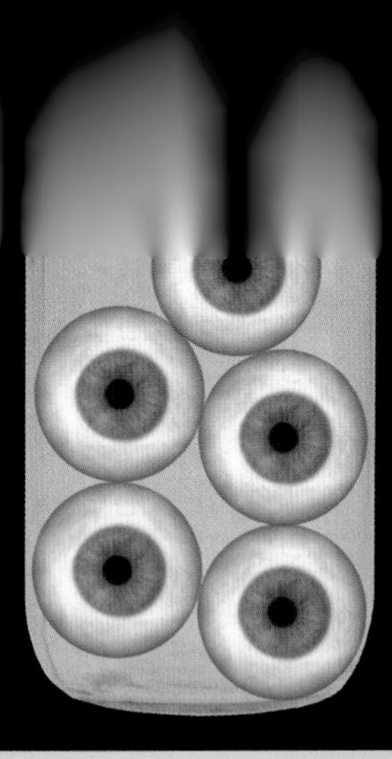

Darwin found that the evolution of the human eye was one of the hardest cases to explain through natural selection. The structure and the way it works is so complex and seemingly so perfect. Despite knowing very little about the eye as compared to scientists' know-how today, Darwin stayed convinced that the human eye had adapted gradually from a simple to a complex organ. Each stage had been useful to the creature, and as the eye varied so the best variations were passed on.

Here's how scientists today think the human eye evolved:

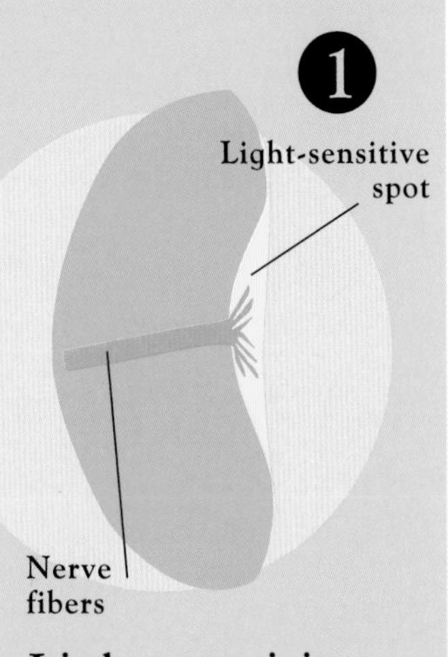

Light-sensitive spot

Some creature in the past had a simple light-sensitive spot on its skin that gave it a slight competitive advantage, perhaps by being able to avoid a predator.

I'm the sea-creature lancelet. My eye is just like your ancestor's.

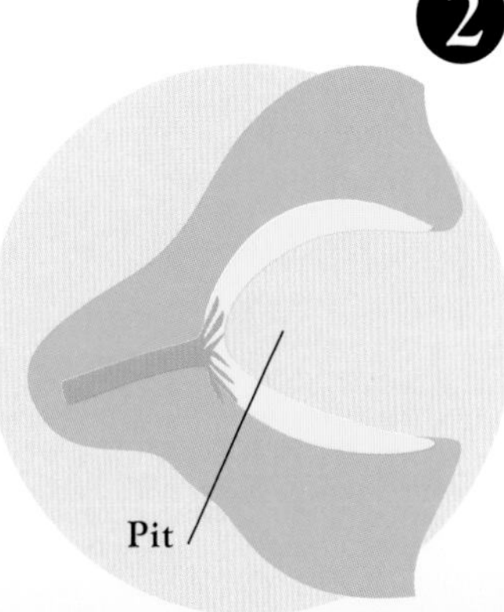

Pinhole

Over time—calculated as 364,000 years by one scientist—a pit in the light-sensitive patch appeared in creatures, providing sharper vision. Maybe at about the same time, the front of the pit gradually narrowed, so light entered through a small hole, rather like the eye of a sea squirt.

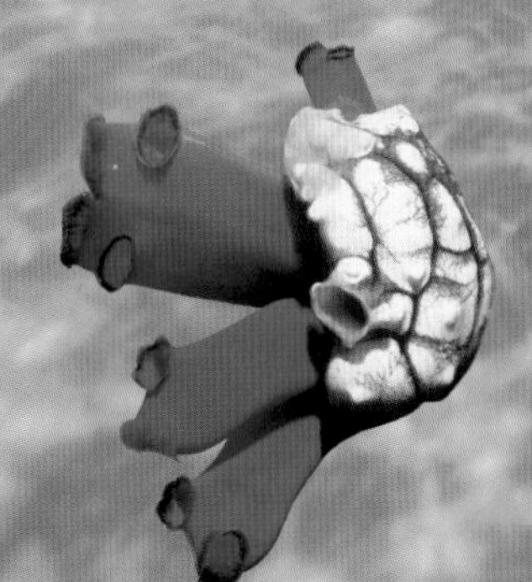

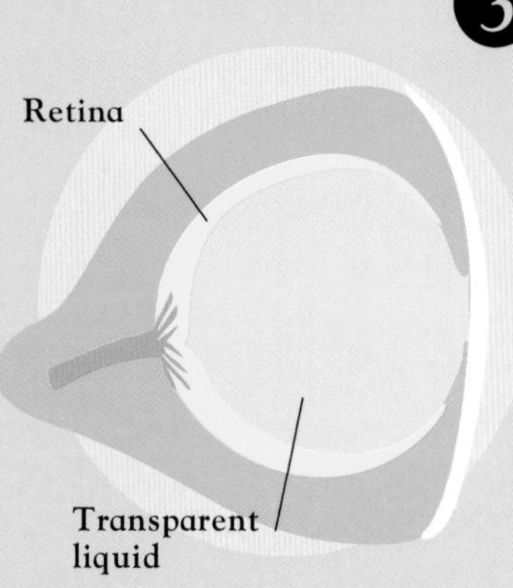

Improved vision

During in-between stages, creatures' eyes developed with an increasing number of cells at the back, a greater curve of the surface, and a slight increase in transparency, rather like the eye of a hagfish.

I'm a hagfish. I can see better in the ocean than that squirt!

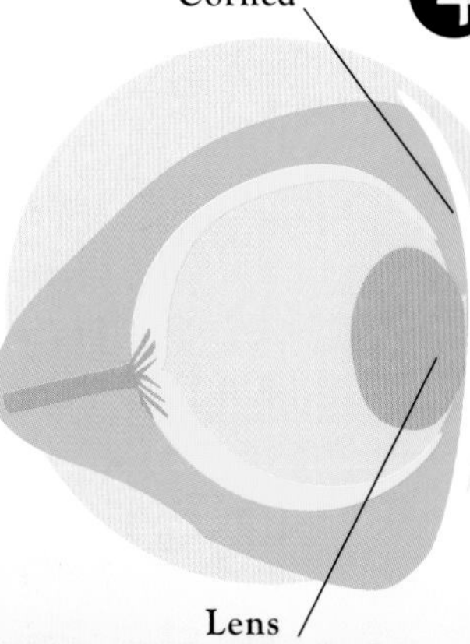

4
Cornea
Lens

Almost perfect

Eventually, the light-sensitive spot at the back became the retina with many cells receiving the image and a lens formed at the front of the eye, making the image clearer on the retina. A lamprey has very similar eyes to ours.

THE WATCHMAKER

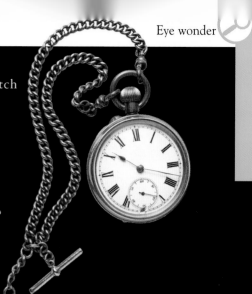

In 1802, clergyman William Paley told a story about chancing upon a watch in a field. The watch had moving parts that worked together for a purpose. He concluded that as the existence of the watch proves that there was a watchmaker, so animals and plants prove the existence of a Creator. Followers of this "natural theology" argued: How could something so marvelous as the human eye have come about only by chance? The eye is complex like a pocket watch so it must have been designed perfectly adapted for its purpose by an intelligent designer.

Not quite the best

5

A human has a single pair of moveable camera-type eyes. The lens can change shape to focus the image onto the back of the eye. But the design is not perfect, since the optic nerve at the back of the eye has to pass through the light-sensitive retina that receives the image, causing a blind spot.

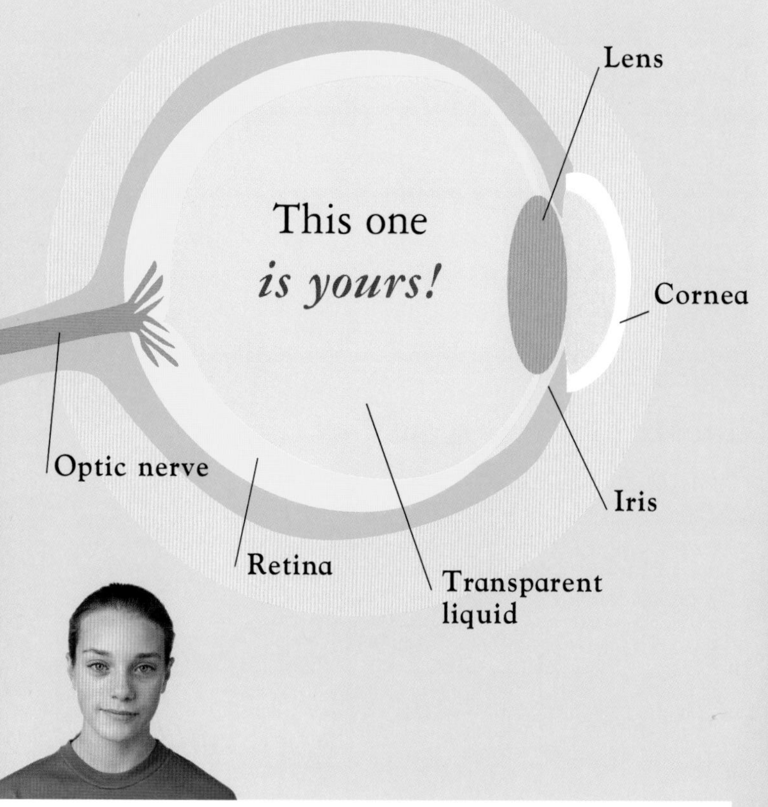

TRY IT YOURSELF: Find your blind spot

Close you left eye and look at the +. Bring the image closer and stop when you can no longer see the ●.

+ ●

Perfection

An octopus has a very similar camera-type eye to a human but it evolved separately and it does have many improvements. There is no blind spot because the nerves come from behind the retina. Another difference is that the lens is a fixed shape but moves closer to the retina to focus.

On the Origin of Species

BESTSELLER

In 1858, Darwin received a letter from young naturalist **Alfred Russel Wallace** that was to force him to publish his secret work of the past 20 years. A year later on November 24, ***1,250 copies*** of a well-written and easy-to-read first edition of his theory of evolution by natural selection were printed, and said to have ***sold out*** on that first day.

A joint presentation

The man in Malaysia

One of Darwin's letter-writing friends was a young man named Alfred Russel Wallace, who was traveling around the islands of Malaysia collecting specimens. In 1858, while recovering from a fever, Wallace had a flash of inspiration as he thought about the animals that lived and died on the islands. In that moment he had come to a similar conclusion as Darwin that the process of natural selection controlled the population size of living things.

Darwin was shocked by the content of Wallace's letter and was at a loss to know what to do. At this time, his ordered family life was in turmoil, since two of his children were very sick. His beloved elder daughter Annie had died seven years earlier and he didn't want to lose another of his dear children. His daughter Henrietta recovered from her illness but unfortunately his youngest son died.

I'll write *a letter to Charlie!* I wonder what he'll make of my idea?
!*?
By Jove! Alfie's *cracked* the theory, too.

Darwin's friends, Lyell and Hooker, came to his aid and organized for a joint presentation of both his and Wallace's essays about evolution to be read to a group of scientists.

READ ALL ABOUT IT!

THE DAILY NEWS

104,000 COPIES SOLD

DARWIN CAUSES A STORM

In 1859, a very public and heated debate between critics and supporters of Charles Darwin's evolution theory erupted on the publication of his book *On the Origin of Species by means of Natural Selection*. But this uproar made everyone want to read it.

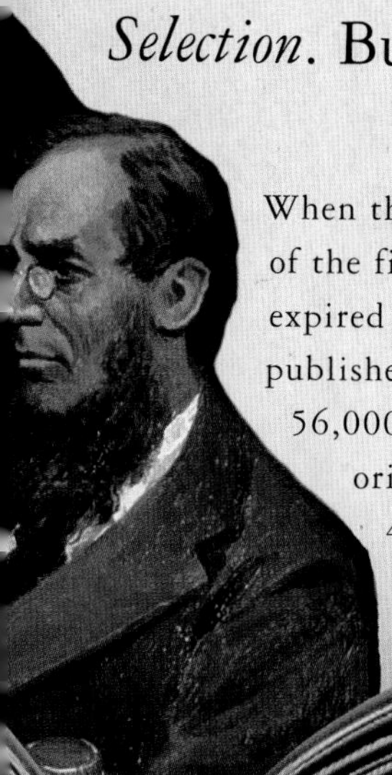

When the copyright of the first edition expired in 1901, the publishers had sold 56,000 copies of the original book and 48,000 copies of a cheap edition covered in paper or cheap cloth. After publication, Darwin said, "I had always feared and predicted an uproar, but I'm delighted about the success of my scientific book."

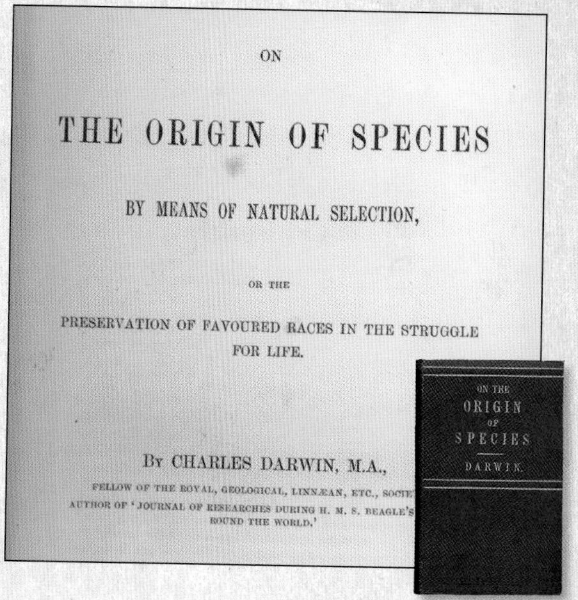

ON

THE ORIGIN OF SPECIES

BY MEANS OF NATURAL SELECTION,

OR THE

PRESERVATION OF FAVOURED RACES IN THE STRUGGLE FOR LIFE.

BY CHARLES DARWIN, M.A.,

FELLOW OF THE ROYAL, GEOLOGICAL, LINNÆAN, ETC., SOCIE

AUTHOR OF 'JOURNAL OF RESEARCHES DURING H. M. S. BEAGLE'S ROUND THE WORLD.'

ON THE ORIGIN OF SPECIES

DARWIN

Darwin outlined his theory of natural selection, justifying it with observations and evidence he had researched. The lengthy full title finally chosen was *On the Origin of Species by means of Natural Selection or the Preservations of Favoured Races in the Struggle for Life*. Editions have been printed all over the world.

Post-ORIGIN

Darwin continued to write a number of other books expanding on different aspects of his theory relating to plants and humans. But, in later life, he chose to specialize again in a detailed project—the actions of earthworms.

KEEP PLAYING! THEY'RE MOVING. HOW FASCINATING!

Worm charming

Darwin thought that worms played a very important role in Earth's history and set out to prove this. One of his experiments involved his whole family playing different instruments to find out how the worms would respond. Darwin found that worms couldn't hear but would react to the vibrations if placed on an instrument.

MMMM, DINNER!

I'M FEELING VIBRATIONS.

IS IT A MOLE COMING? LET'S GET OUT OF HERE!

QUICK! IS IT RAINING? I LOVE THE WET.

NOW TRY THIS: Stick a garden fork into the soil and gently rock it to and fro. You'll notice earthworms coming to the surface.

TRUE or *false*

There have been a number of inaccurate statements made about Darwin's life and work. Below are a handful of some of these misconceptions to set the record straight:

Darwin came up with his **theory of evolution** while at the ***Galápagos Islands.***

False. His ideas came later after his return from the voyage.

The ***title*** of Darwin's book is "Origin of the species."

False. By adding the "the" it implies that Darwin wrote about the origins of a particular species, which was not what the book is about.

Darwin came up with the phrase "survival of the fittest" to summarize his theory.

False. The philosopher Herbert Spencer coined this phrase.

Darwin said, ***"humans came from monkeys."***

False. Darwin wrote only that monkeys, apes, and humans must have a common ancestor.

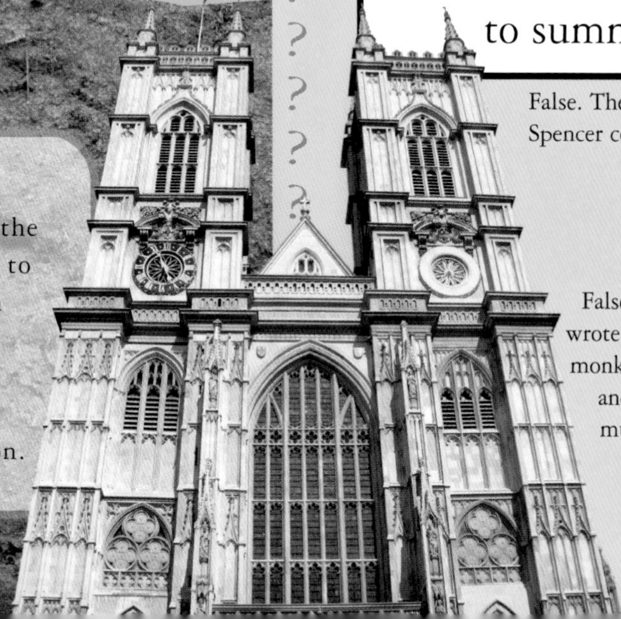

A hero's burial

When Darwin died in 1882, the scientific community wanted to honor him. Although Darwin had only requested a quiet funeral, his body was buried in a great ceremony at Westminster Abbey in London.

RIP

SQUEAK! YOU AND I HAVE THE SAME NUMBER OF GENES. LET'S BE FRIENDS!

ALL IN THE GENES

Today, we know something that Darwin had no idea about—genetics. By studying the microscopic chemical codes passed down from generation to generation, scientists have increased their understanding of how species have evolved.

We can now explain what makes us all unique and even trace ourselves back to common ancestors we share with other odd-looking creatures.

Not only does Darwin's natural selection theory hold up to this scientific scrutiny, but geneticists have also discovered other laws at work in nature. Their findings have also raised a number of ethical issues and aspects of evolution continue to cause very heated debates.

The pea plant puzzle

Hidden away in a monastery garden, a 19th-century Austrian monk, Gregor Mendel, was trying out experiments on pea plants. His tests were revealing that features were being passed down in many pieces of information from the parent plants to their offspring. We now call these pieces "genes."

Traits and characteristics

A trait is a feature and characteristics are the many forms of that feature. For example, the trait studied in this test is pod color and the characteristics are either yellow or green.

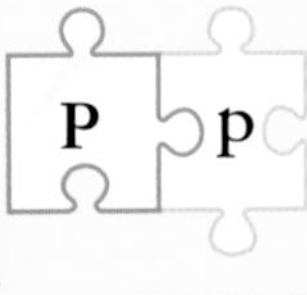

P p

These pieces represent the gene for the pea pod color. P for green pods and p for yellow pods.

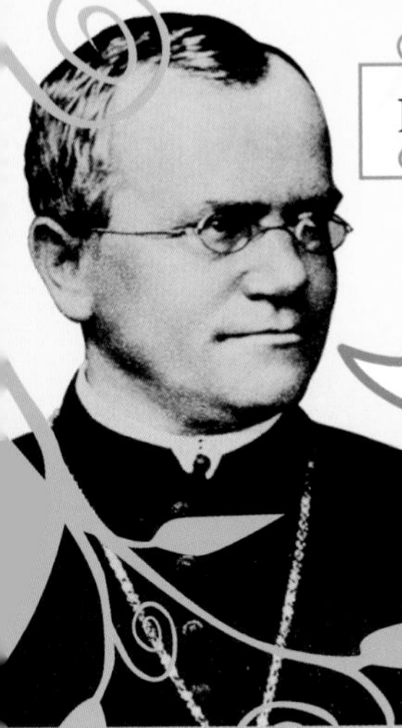

That's interesting! If the offspring get both a P and p piece then the plant shows the P feature. This copy must be stronger.

Gregor Mendel (1822–1884)

Test results

Mendel rubbed the pollen (male part) of one plant onto the stigma (female part) of the other plant.

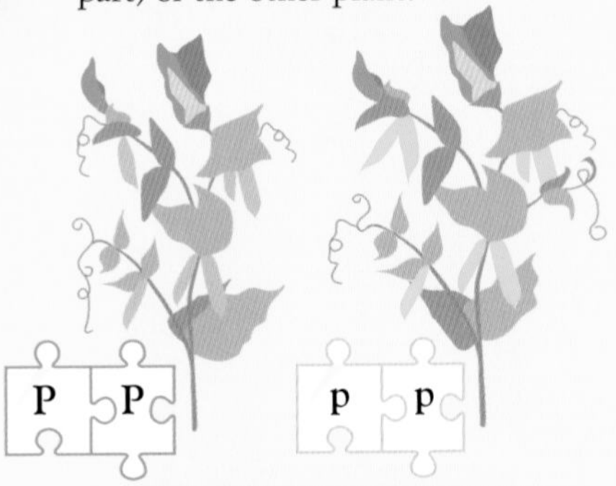

P P   p p

The offspring have two copies of each gene—one from each parent.

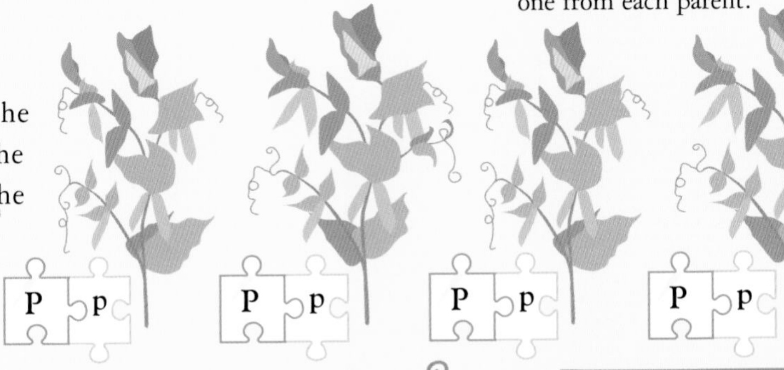

P p   P p   P p   P p

How the two copies mix determines the pod color.

P P   p p   P p   P p

Chromosomes

Under the microscope, scientists looking into the cells of plants and animals discovered that the middle part, the nucleus, contained a number of threadlike shapes. These became known as chromosomes.

Different CHROMOSOMES contain different GENES.

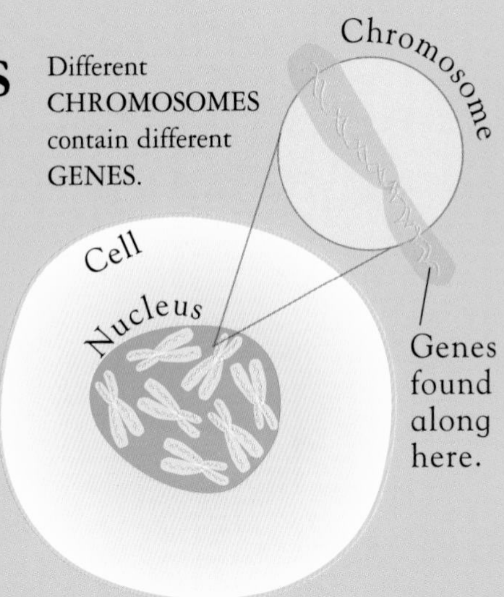

Chromosome

Cell

Nucleus

Genes found along here.

Different LIVING THINGS have a different number of CHROMOSOMES.

The number does not have any connection with the complexity of the life form.

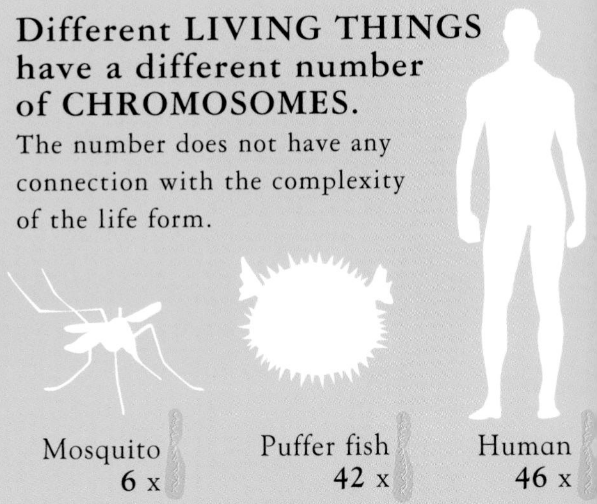

Mosquito 6 x

Puffer fish 42 x

Human 46 x

If Mendel met Darwin

Although these two great guys never met, if they had, maybe their conversation would have gone like this:

MENDEL: Great idea about natural selection, Charles. God certainly moves in mysterious ways!

DARWIN: Thanks. It's surprising that no one had come up with the idea before. Mind you, I'm still not certain about how inheritance works.

MENDEL: Maybe I can help you with this. I've been doing some breeding experiments on pea plants. The results have been most interesting.

DARWIN: I found testing plants a useful way of finding out about something, too. Tell me about your tests.

MENDEL: Well, I placed the pollen from a pea plant with green pods on to the female part of a pea plant with yellow pods.

DARWIN: Did the offspring all have greenish-yellow pods?

MENDEL: No. All the offspring had green pods.

DARWIN: Oh! So the physical appearances were not a blend of the parents' characteristics.

MENDEL: That's right. I'm thinking that these "characters" were passed down from each parent unchanged. In each offspring, the characters from each parent separate and join with one set of the characters of the other parent. In this test, the stronger character—the green color pod—appeared in all the offspring. That's not all!

DARWIN: What did you do next?

MENDEL: Well, I took the pollen from one offspring and placed it on the female part of another offspring. And you'd never guess the result?

DARWIN: All the offspring had green pods again.

MENDEL: No! Most of these offspring did have green pods, but there were a few with yellow pods. Imagine my surprise.

DARWIN: Well, why do you think that happened?

MENDEL: I propose that tiny pieces of hereditary information are being passed down unchanged from generation to generation. This means that a weaker character—the yellow color pod—that has been masked in one generation can reappear unchanged in another.

DARWIN: What else do you know about these pieces?

MENDEL: There's a piece for each of the traits determining seed shape, seed size, flower color, pod shape, pod size, stem height, and so on. I've studied more than one trait at a time in the pea plants and noticed that, for example, the piece for pod color is sorted separately from the piece for pod shape in each individual offspring.

DARWIN: Good work, Gregor. I wonder what these pieces look like and how they are linked together?

MENDEL: I'll have to leave that for future scientists to discover.

Dog
78 x

Goldfish
94 x

Human chromosomes are arranged in pairs, which are all matching except for the pair of sex chromosomes of a male. Chromosomes vary in size and shape depending on the number of genes they contain. Scientists arrange the pairs in order of size on a chart called a karyotype.

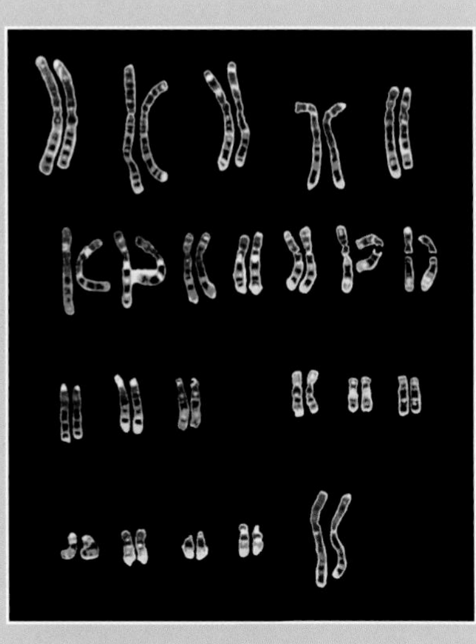

FEMALE HUMAN KARYOTYPE

Every body cell in a living thing contains the same number of chromosomes. Cells pass on their chromosomes when they divide to produce new cells. Every chromosome makes an exact copy of itself and then divides to make a new cell.

Genetic recipe

Instructions on how to build a living thing:

The packages: The hereditary material is divided into a number of packages called chromosomes, which are found inside every cell.

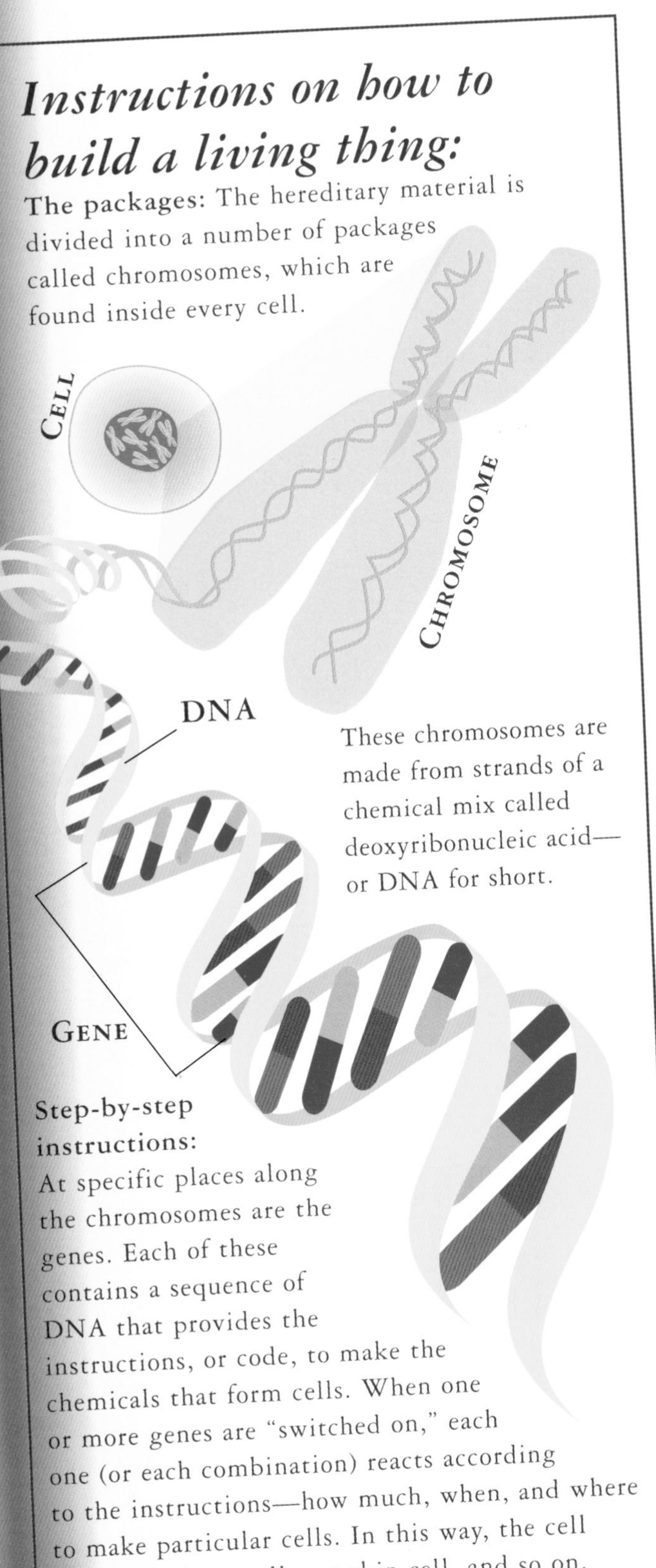

These chromosomes are made from strands of a chemical mix called deoxyribonucleic acid—or DNA for short.

Step-by-step instructions: At specific places along the chromosomes are the genes. Each of these contains a sequence of DNA that provides the instructions, or code, to make the chemicals that form cells. When one or more genes are "switched on," each one (or each combination) reacts according to the instructions—how much, when, and where to make particular cells. In this way, the cell becomes a lung cell or a skin cell, and so on.

Mind-boggling and extremely complex investigations have been undertaken by scientists since the start of the 20th century to seek the complete picture of genetics (the study of heredity). But how does this help us to understand evolution?

The genome

The big picture revealed so far is that all a living thing's inherited material is wrapped up in a genome. This is the ***instruction manual*** containing most of the basic information needed for building an individual.

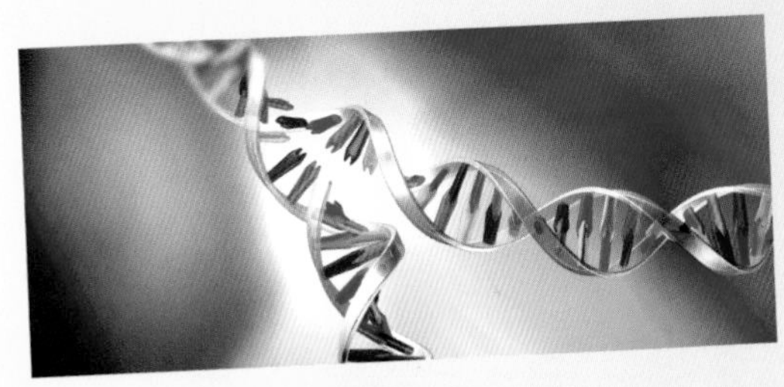

The spiral ladder

The structure of DNA is shaped like a spiral ladder. The rungs make up a simple code represented by the four letters A, C, G, and T (shown as blue, red, yellow, and green), which stand for the base chemicals. Each rung has a pair of bases that splits in the middle when making an exact copy of itself for new cells.

Extract your DNA

Ask an adult for permission and help

You will need:
• a glass of salty water • a glass with 1 tsp dishwashing liquid • 3 tsp tap water • a clean teaspoon • 4 fl oz (125 ml) ice-cold alcohol (gin or vodka that's been in the freezer is ideal)

1. Swill the salty water around your mouth. ***Do not swallow.***

2. Spit the contents of your mouth into the glass containing the dishwashing liquid and tap water. Stir slowly with the clean teaspoon for a couple of minutes.

3. ***Very slowly*** pour the ice-cold alcohol down the inside of the glass so that it settles on top of the solution.
Leave for 2–3 minutes.

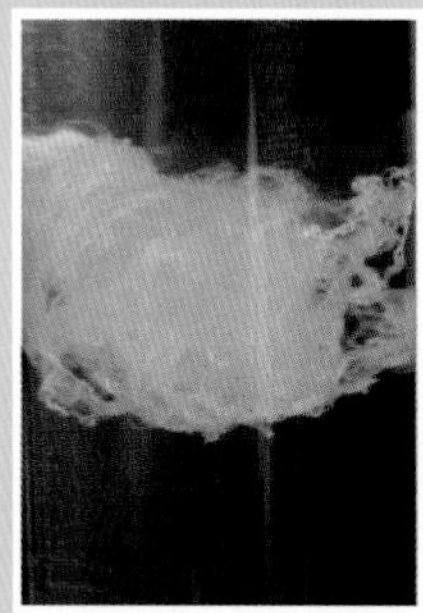

4. Observe the thin strands on top of the salty detergent mixture. This is your DNA.

If you wish, carefully remove the strand by twisting a plastic straw slowly in the glass. The strands will wrap around it, but they are very fragile. Once extracted you could stain the strands with food coloring to make them easier to see under a microscope.

Throw away the DNA and the liquid in the glass after use.

Mapping the genome

In 1990, an ambitious project involving many international scientists began to map out the complete sequence of the human genome. It took them 13 years to unravel the information for 3 billion rungs of the DNA ladder and identify the estimated 25,000 genes and where they were located. This team of scientists have also mapped the genomes of yeast, a roundworm, a mouse, and a fruit fly. Impressive! But, the findings raised more questions than answers.

There are a number of genes for which the uses are unknown. Some genes look a lot like genes found in very different living things, such as fish.

Why do the sizes of genomes vary so much between different species?

There's so much other stuff in DNA besides genes. What is it for and why do other living things have less of this "junk"?

DNA and evolution

Thanks to understanding more about DNA, these strands of hereditary material provide the strongest proof for biological evolution—how genetic changes were made over time to make new species. By comparing the genomes of different living things and observing the changes in the coding of the genes, scientists can figure out how closely different species relate to each other and even identify how long ago a common ancestor lived.

Humans have the same number of genes as mice. We carry the gene for making a tail but it gets switched off early in development. 90% of the genes linked to diseases are the same, which is why mice are so valuable for use in lab research on human illness.

Our genomes are 96% **IDENTICAL to a human's.** Our differences are possibly due to where and when the genes have been switched on in the brain.

550 million years ago humans had a common ancestor with the lancelet, a rod-like sea animal (see it on page 34).

All this thinking is making me hungry. Pass that banana!

We share about 31% of our genes with YEAST—a single living cell that replicates every 90 minutes.

We share 50% of our genes with a BANANA.

One in a *quintillion*

46 CHROMOSOMES IN PAIRS

This grandma has green eyes.

46 CHROMOSOMES IN PAIRS

This granddad has blue eyes.

Your parents would have to have another 1,000,000,000,000,000 babies before one possibly might have the same genes as you. This genetic variation between individuals is the key to how species have evolved.

46 CHROMOSOMES IN PAIRS

This grandad has green eyes.

46 CHROMOSOMES IN PAIRS

This grandma has brown eyes.

Each parent's 46 chromosomes are shuffled, divided, and half (23) are passed on to a child.

23 CHROMOSOMES

23 CHROMOSOMES

Chip off the old block

Your appearance, your fingerprints, your voice, your health, and even how you clasp your hands have been coded by your genes. These genes have been passed down from your parents, who received their genes from their parents, who received their genes from their parents, and so on. You might have similar features to a family ancestor that have skipped a few generations. So how has this variation between us all happened?

46 CHROMOSOMES IN PAIRS

This dad has green eyes.

23 CHROMOSOMES

Answer: Half of your chromosomes that contain the genes have come from your mother and the other half from your father. Which half of their chromosomes you get and how these two sets of chromosomes come together is what makes you so unique, even from any brothers and sisters (unless you have an identical twin).

23 CHROMOSOMES

23 CHROMOSOMES

46 CHROMOSOMES IN PAIRS

This mom has brown eyes.

23 CHROMOSOMES

Studying twins

Identical twins have the same genes. By studying their traits, scientists have been able to figure out which ones their genes have influenced and which their environment and upbringing have affected. Results have shown that genes affect appearance, eyesight, weight, IQ, and length of life, but have less influence on food preferences and sense of humor.

Boy or girl?

Two of your chromosomes contain a gene that determines what sex you will be. These sex chromosomes are shaped like the letters X and Y. If you are a girl you have received an X-chromosome from both your parents, but if you are a boy you have one X-chromosome from your mother and one Y-chromosome from your father. For boys, all the genes on the X-chromosome are dominant since there is no matching pair, which means they might inherit genetic disorders from their mother. For example, color blindness is a recessive gene that becomes dominant when passed on from mother to son.

Can you see a number in this circle of colored dots? If not, you might be color blind. Test your family.

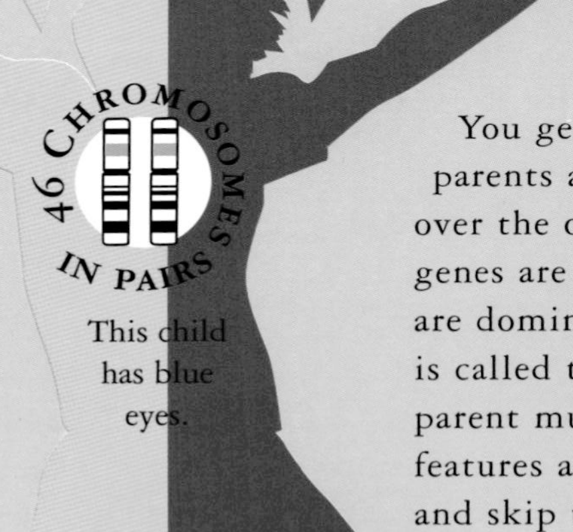

This child has blue eyes.

HUMAN GENETICS like those of many other living things is not as simple as one gene for each trait. Often one gene can affect several traits or several genes can affect one trait, such as height or eye color.

You get a set of genes affecting eye color from both parents and if they are different then one set gets priority over the other—this is called the **DOMINANT**. Brown-eye genes are usually dominant over green-eye genes, which are dominant over blue-eye genes. The weaker of the set is called the **RECESSIVE**. To get the recessive feature, each parent must pass on a copy of the weaker genes. Often these features appear in grandparents and their grandchildren and skip their parents.

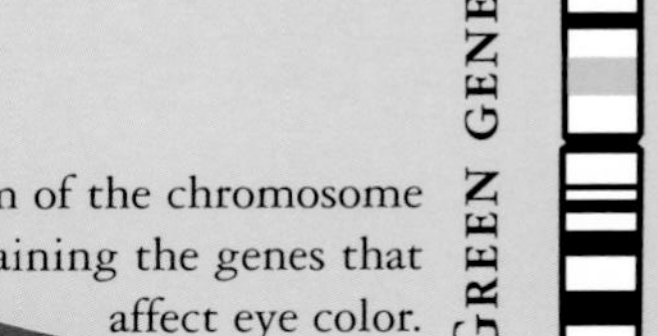

Diagram of the chromosome containing the genes that affect eye color.

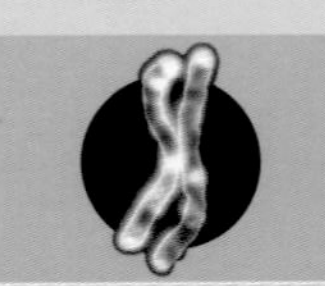
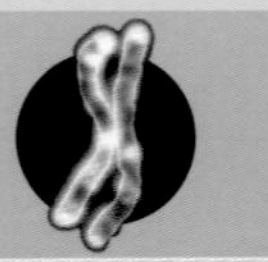
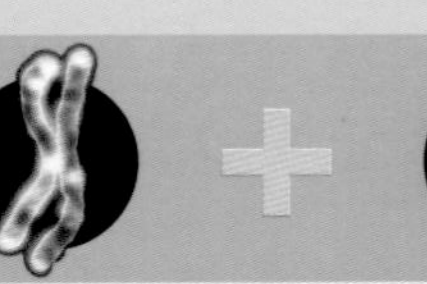
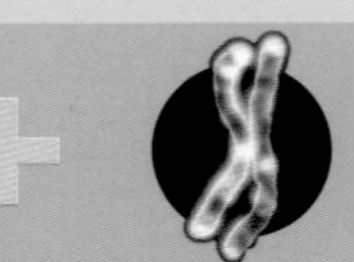
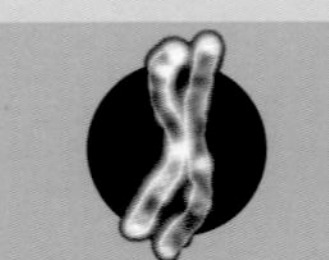

WHEN THE CHROMOSOMES COME TOGETHER TO FORM YOU, THERE ARE TWO SETS OF EVERY GENE.

NOW TRY THIS! *Take the genes test to discover what you might have inherited.*

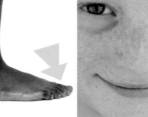

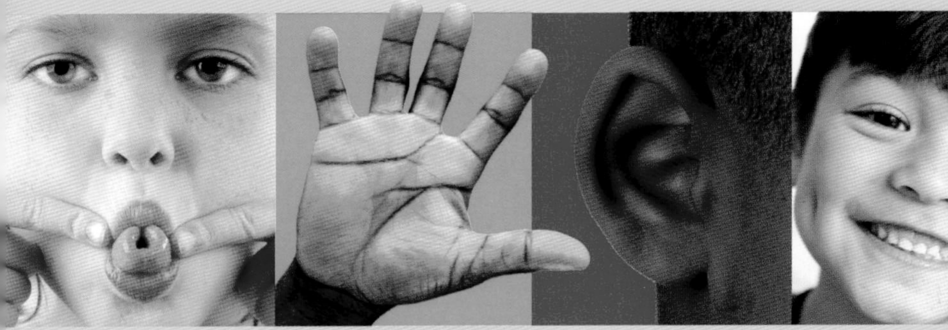
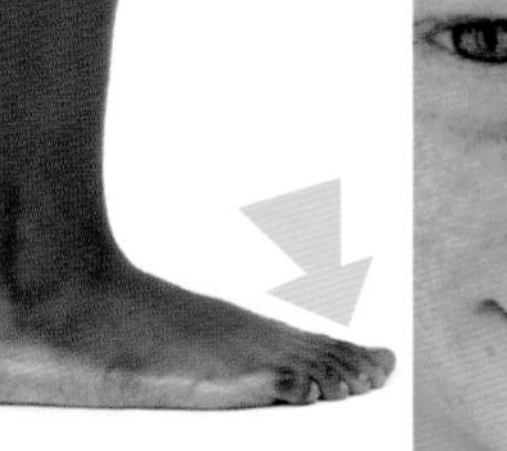
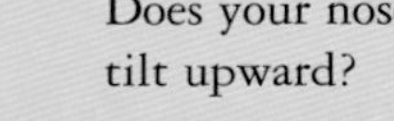

Can you roll your tongue into a U-shape?

Does the top part of your little finger bend in toward the next finger?

Does your earlobe hang free at the bottom?

Do you have dimples in your cheeks when you smile?

Can you bend your thumb back more than 30°?

Does hair grow on the middle part of your toes?

Do you have freckles?

Does your nose tilt upward?

Now test your family and relatives. Record their answers and trace the genes through your family tree.

Every now and then, DNA within an individual's cells can become altered or damaged. These **random errors** are called **mutations**. When the changed DNA is passed on to their offspring, this causes genetic variation, which might be ***naturally selected*** for the **EVOLUTION** of a species.

Winners or losers?

Mutations are rare but over time they build up to have an effect. Inherited mutations can either have *no effect* on the individual, or have a *harmful* effect on the individual, or give the individual a *competitive advantage*. Through natural selection, the individual will either go on to breed and pass on its mutation or die and the mutation discontinues.

Neutral

Siamese cats have a mutated gene that causes kittens to be white at birth and then later to develop patches of color at certain points on their faces, paws, and tails.

Helpful

Tigers have a mutated gene that gave them stripes. In the past, those with this gene were able to blend into the tall grasses and be more successful at catching food and surviving, so the mutated gene passed on to their offspring.

Home, sweet home

Whether a mutation is selected as harmful or helpful to individuals depends on their environment. In Antarctica, the sea is the best place to get food, so penguins have evolved through many small mutations to have webbed feet and stunted wings, perfect for swimming fast to catch food and escaping predators.

I've forgotten how to fly.

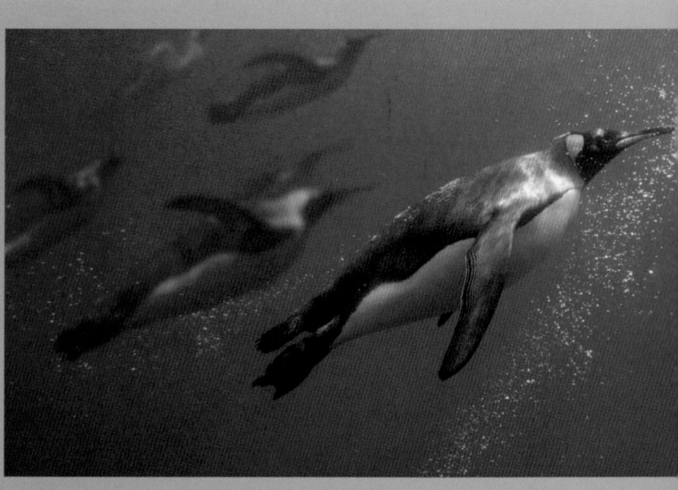

Inherited mutation *creates*  genetic variation *acted on by*

Who gets what?

Mutations can be inherited either from one parent or both parents, depending on whether the change is on recessive (weak) or dominant (priority) genes. There's a 50% chance of inheriting a mutated dominant gene carried by one parent. However, there's only a 25% chance of inheriting a mutated recessive gene and even that depends on both parents being carriers.

My ancestors came from the Isle of Man.
M
M
M

Harmful

Manx cats carry a mutated gene that causes many kittens to be stillborn or die within their first year if inherited from both parents. If they only inherit the gene from one parent then the kittens do survive, but many have stumpy tails or no tails.

The Manx gene is dominant. Cats that carry the gene (M) pass it on to half their offspring.

However, these mutations are useless on land. Penguins would be unable to survive in an environment without water.

WHAT CAN GO WRONG?

DNA can get altered

when cells are dividing and the copying process of the chromosomes goes wrong. A gene could be copied wrongly. If a chromosome breaks or an extra gap appears in the DNA sequence, a gene is unlikely to work. When an extra chromosome number 21 appears in a cell, this mutation causes physical and mental differences known as Down's syndrome.

DNA can be broken

when radiation or chemicals affect the body and the cells are unable to repair themselves completely. If this damage affects the reproductive cells then the mutation could be inherited. As humans spread around the world, the amount and quality of sunlight (ultraviolet radiation) absorbed by the cells altered the DNA of the skin color gene.

UV radiation causes a bulge in the DNA sequence

Sections of DNA can move

to another position on the chromosomes, often causing gene mutations. The color patterns in maize are due to these "jumping" genes.

Moveable sections of DNA either copy themselves so there are duplicate copies on the chromosomes or are "cut and pasted" from one chromosome to another, as shown here.

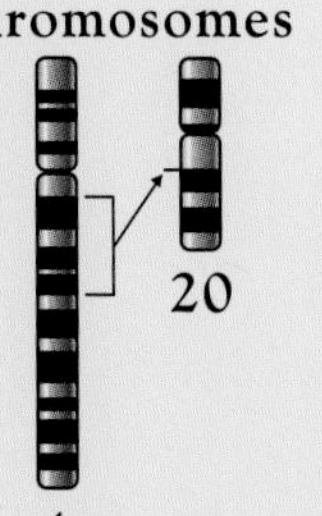

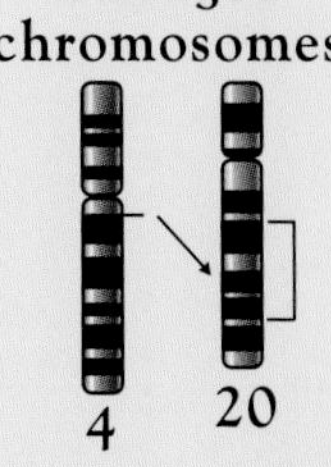

> natural selection = evolution of species

WE'RE ALL

All living things are mutants, including us, since we have all evolved from mutated genes, setting us apart from each other. Some mutated genes cause rare conditions and these get carried along, hidden within the DNA sequence of "carrier" individuals. Every now and then, when a carrier or carriers have offspring, the condition reappears.

Ghostly

The genes affecting skin, hair, or feather color have been mutated to reduce the amount of pigment (color) in a condition called leucism. The animal appears white, which means it can be spotted easily by prey and predators.

Hairless

Some people have a human hairless gene, which means they lose all their hair very quickly after birth. They not only have no hair on their head, but also have no eyebrows, no eyelashes, no nasal hair, and no body hair. They need extra protection from the sun and bacteria.

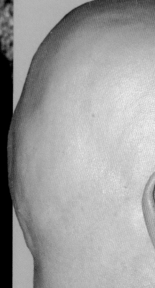

Better than one?

In the early stages as a developing embryo (egg), this snake started out as twins, but then due to a gene defect stopped, leaving two heads on one body. Often the two heads disagree and might even try to swallow each other.

MUTANTS

Extra digits

A gene for six digits causes the cells making the fingers or toes during early development to keep working. It's a dominant gene so it takes priority, but it's also extremely rare.

I'm Stumpy.
I'm famous for being born with two extra legs in February, 2007.

Now try this!

Draw a picture or use a photograph of yourself. Change three of your features by changing the size or the color, adding more, or removing.

Can you think of any situations in which these mutations might be naturally selected to give you a competitive advantage?

For example, make your thumbs larger to help you move the games console controls faster. This inherited mutation might be naturally selected as a useful adaptation in a technology-driven environment.

NOT IMPOSSIBLE! A PANDA'S THUMB IS AN ENLARGED WRIST BONE—A MUTATION THAT WAS NATURALLY SELECTED SINCE IT GIVES THE ANIMAL AN EXCELLENT GRIP ON ITS FAVORITE FOOD, BAMBOO.

Twists of fortune...

Ready for another evolutionary bombshell that Darwin didn't consider? Natural selection is not the only process affecting *which genes make it* through to the next generation. Completely at RANDOM,

KEY

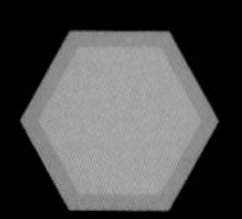 = This shape represents the changing size of the gene pool of the red kite species.

1 The total of all the genes of a species is called the gene pool. This includes all the many variations of all the genes.

This is the story of the red kite species, so far. Populations of the red kite ranged across North and Central Europe and North Africa.

2 The gene pool INCREASES when a mutated gene survives. Natural selection is at work, selecting the variations that are best adapted to the environment.

Red kites are predators and scavengers and evolved impressive wingspans and excellent eyesight, enabling them to find animal carcasses on the ground.

3 The gene pool also INCREASES when new genes are introduced. This happens when different populations breed with each other. This transfer of genes is called *gene flow*.

European populations of red kites followed migration patterns south across Europe to North Africa and back. Individuals from the different populations would breed with each other.

4 The gene pool DECREASES when animals die or don't breed. The random process of genetic drift might be more noticeable in a small population, reducing the number of genetic variations.

Since the 1500s, the red kites in Britain were considered pests and were being killed. As the kite became rare, many were caught and stuffed for collections. By the late 1800s, populations of red kites in England and Scotland were extinct and only a handful of pairs were left in remote parts of Wales.

NATURAL SELECTION + GENETIC DRIFT

or fate

some genetic variations make it through while others don't and are lost forever. This process is called **genetic drift** and is more noticeable when it occurs in small populations.

THE FUTURE

8 **The process of natural selection** continues, selecting the most advantageous genetic variations.

The populations in the wild have increased in number and continue to breed successfully. The trait to migrate has been inherited, which means there is a future possibility of further gene flow.

7 **Conserving a species** does not just increase the population size but also creates a gene pool with many variations by introducing individuals from other populations, giving more chance of survival.

During the 1990s, red kites from Sweden, Spain, Germany, and Wales were released into suitable habitats in Scotland and England.

Sometimes a kite from the Welsh population is born with white feathers. Rare, often harmful, mutations become more evident in populations that have been through a genetic bottleneck.

5 **When species drop** to very low numbers and then increases again, they are said to pass through a ***genetic bottleneck***.

In the 1930s, the number of red kites was so low that only one female bird remained. The population slowly increased but all were her descendants.

6 **Species close to extinction** face a number of problems due to having a small gene pool.

The habitat of the Welsh red kites had a harsh climate and a limited food supply. The population recovered slowly during the mid-1900s because of pesticides and a disease that killed their rabbit prey.

9 **Random events** may wipe out individuals with selectively advantageous genes. The lottery of which genes make it through continues.

Kites are being killed or injured by the blades of wind turbines and poisoned by the illegal poison baits left out for foxes and crows, and by eating poisoned rats. One kite has been killed by colliding with a jet fighter aircraft.

= SIZE OF GENE POOL

Mystery of *mysteries*

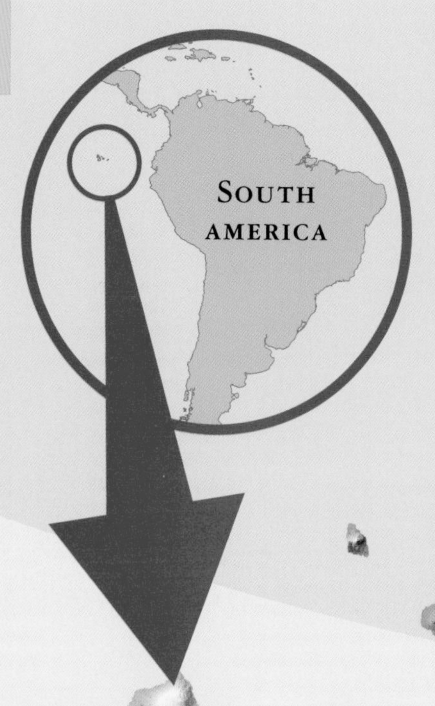

How do new species form? Darwin referred to this question as "the mystery of mysteries." There are many explanations of how this process called speciation works, but most scientists agree that on islands, geographical isolation is a major factor. The many species of finches of the Galápagos Islands are famous for being studied by Darwin, but they continue to be an excellent example of how new species evolve.

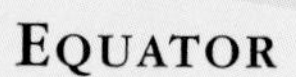

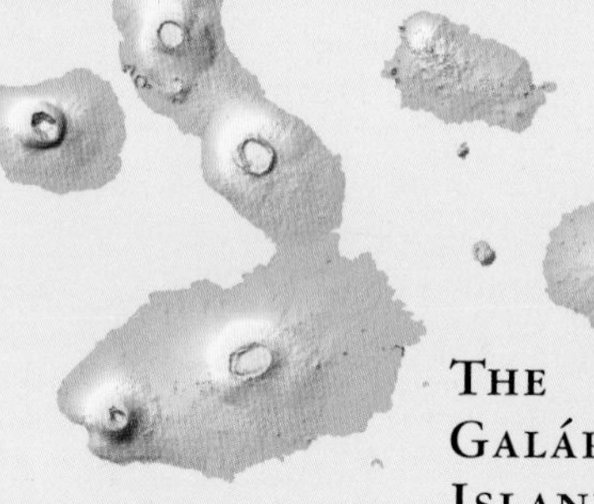

Separation

Around three million years ago, a group of ground finches from South America was blown across to an island in the Galápagos. Separated from their own population, these seed-eating birds arrived in a cloud-forest habitat that was full of different things to eat. Their descendants gradually adapted to occupy their own niche. Their body size changed as some moved from the ground to the trees and their beak shape changed as some fed on fruit, nectar, insects, or spiders.

Adaptation

Over the last three million years, the Galápagos islands have changed. New islands have appeared, the climate has become more varied, and so the food sources—plants and animals—have changed, too. Although weak fliers, the finches have been blown to other islands and adapted to fill a niche in their new situations.

Speciation is like some characters in a story going off on an adventure that changes their looks

A new species is achieved when *two populations of the same living thing* become so ***different*** that they can **NO LONGER SUCCESSFULLY BREED WITH EACH OTHER.**

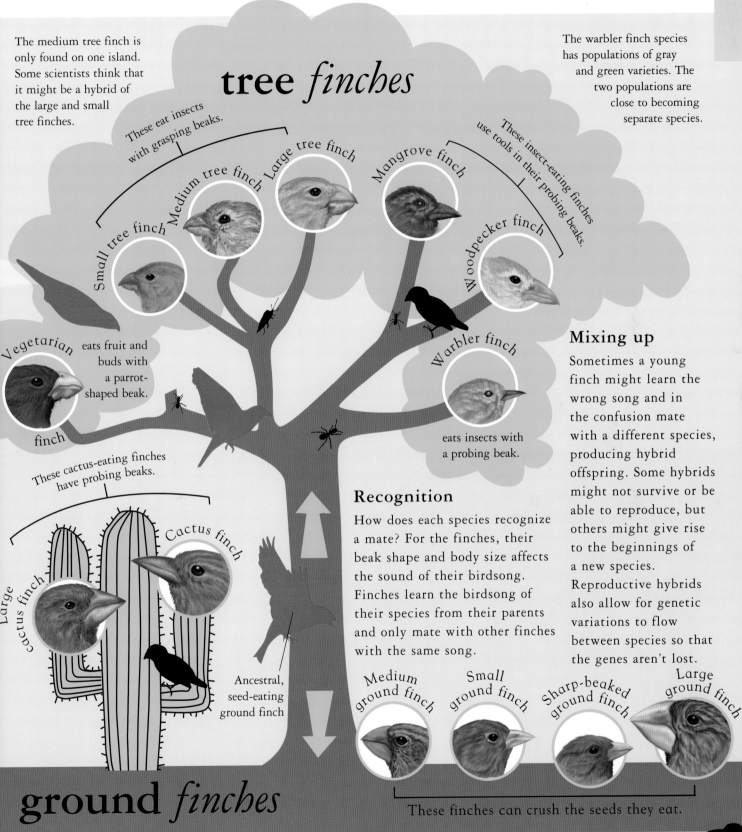

The medium tree finch is only found on one island. Some scientists think that it might be a hybrid of the large and small tree finches.

The warbler finch species has populations of gray and green varieties. The two populations are close to becoming separate species.

tree *finches*

These eat insects with grasping beaks.

Small tree finch

Medium tree finch

Large tree finch

These insect-eating finches use tools in their probing beaks.

Mangrove finch

Woodpecker finch

Vegetarian finch

eats fruit and buds with a parrot-shaped beak.

Warbler finch

eats insects with a probing beak.

These cactus-eating finches have probing beaks.

Large cactus finch

Cactus finch

Ancestral, seed-eating ground finch

Recognition

How does each species recognize a mate? For the finches, their beak shape and body size affects the sound of their birdsong. Finches learn the birdsong of their species from their parents and only mate with other finches with the same song.

Mixing up

Sometimes a young finch might learn the wrong song and in the confusion mate with a different species, producing hybrid offspring. Some hybrids might not survive or be able to reproduce, but others might give rise to the beginnings of a new species. Reproductive hybrids also allow for genetic variations to flow between species so that the genes aren't lost.

Medium ground finch

Small ground finch

Sharp-beaked ground finch

Large ground finch

These finches can crush the seeds they eat.

ground *finches*

and behavior so much that when they return home, they are no longer recognized.

A GHOST in

WOOOOOOOOOOo

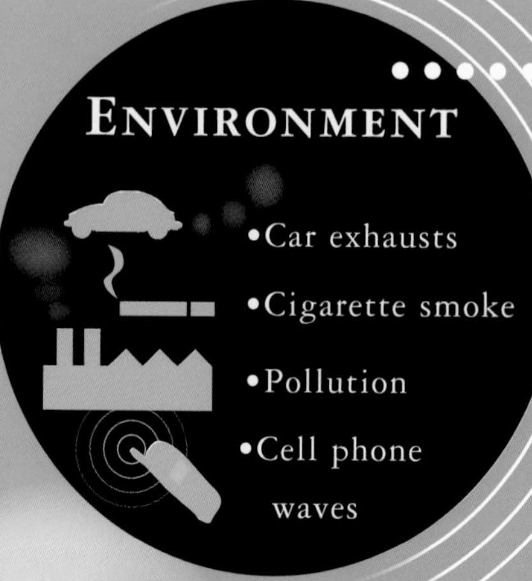

ENVIRONMENT
•Car exhausts
•Cigarette smoke
•Pollution
•Cell phone waves

Genes remember the past.

This is the theory some scientists have recently suggested. The lives of your grandparents when they were growing up—the air they breathed, the food they ate, how they felt, and the things they saw—affect your health and behavior, and how you live your life will affect your grandchildren. It's not just DNA we're inheriting, but these influences tagging along on top of it.

YOU ARE... what your grandparents breathed in. A grandparent's exposure to an industrial poison may be the cause of a certain cancer in their grandchildren.

What we do to our bodies...

could affect **our** grandchildren—how happy they will be, how much they eat, and what diseases they may get.

your *genes*

EMOTION

- *Love*
- HATE
- *Stress*
- CALM
- **Hardship**

FOOD AND DRINK

- Refined sugar
- Pesticides on food
- Alcohol

- Canned drinks
- Additives

CHEMICALS

- Spray-on creams
- Injections
- Drugs, including medicines

YOU ARE...

what your grandparents ate. The amount of food our grandparents ate affects whether our genes will be able to cope with how much or how little we eat. If they ate well, then we are more likely to live longer if we eat well than if we eat less.

THE SWITCHBOARD

Every cell carries the entire genetic code in its DNA. Switching genes on and off affects what that cell will be used for—a lung cell, a skin cell, a brain cell, an eye cell, and so on.

What's controlling the switches?

DNA contains the instruction code for controlling genes, but it can be affected by chemical tags that override the DNA instructions. These tags add up over a lifetime and are caused by lifestyle habits. Tags not only cause immediate changes but may also be inherited by the next generation.

These tags cause changes by hiding certain genes, switching them off, which makes another gene switch on instead. Faulty switches cause health and behavior problems, such as obesity (overweight), diabetes (too much sugar in blood), mental illness, cancers (when the cells divide too quickly), and heart disease.

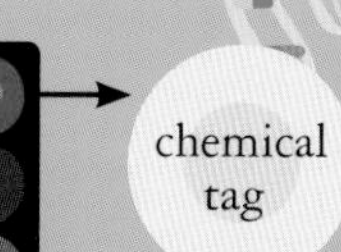

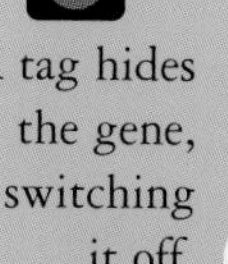

A tag hides the gene, switching it off.

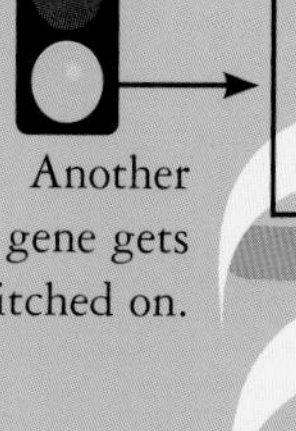

Another gene gets switched on.

Scientists are studying whether they can control these switches. If so, maybe one day they can switch diseased cells back to being normal.

Does this theory sound familiar? Remember Chevalier de Lamarck from page 13 and his idea that animals were changed within their lifetime by their environment? He had a good idea but used the wrong examples!

Honeybees, army ants, and social wasps belong to a group of insects that form large and highly organized colonies. Evolution is driven by individuals successfully passing on their genes to the next generation. However, these colonies have only a few individuals that have offspring and the rest just work to look after the offspring. So why have colonies evolved?

Each individual has a job to do within the colony.

A queen mates with many males over several days to get a good mix of genes. Then over many years she lays a mix of fertilized and unfertilized eggs.

The fertilized eggs become the female bees, of which most will be the workers, and the unfertilized eggs become the male bees, called drones.

Workers perform *a waggle dance* to direct other workers to where they have found food. A gene is thought to control the change in behavior during the life of the worker.

MALE DRONE

Young workers feed the larvae and tend the nest. They control how many female larvae are fed royal jelly to become queen bees and how many male larvae survive.

After three weeks, the workers leave the nest to gather food. Older workers collect pollen and nectar.

But are the workers doing their job for the good of

Family fortunes

WHY might a bird stay in a nest to help care for their parents' next brood as the young male white-fronted African bee eater does?

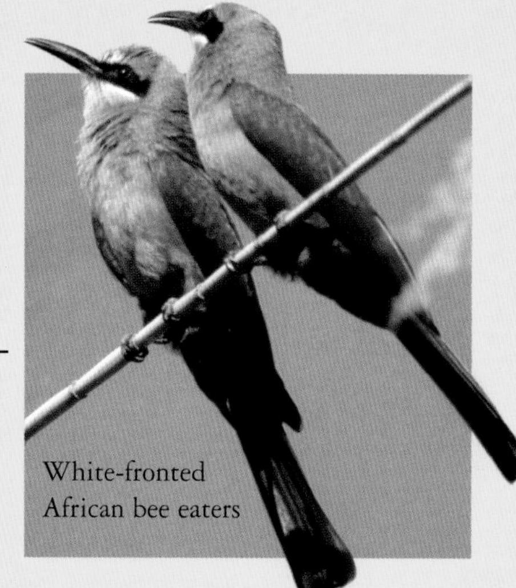
White-fronted African bee eaters

This type of self-sacrificing behavior occurs in a number of groups of animals. The behavior improves survival rates of relatives' offspring. But is this for the good of the family or is there a hidden motive? An individual shares 50% of its genes with each parent and with its brothers and sisters, and has 25% in common with nieces and nephews. By helping the group, the individual is ensuring that many of its genes survive. It also might learn some good parenting skills before having a family of its own.

Super sisters

Why don't worker honeybees have offspring? Unusually, male bees come from unfertilized eggs so have only half (16) the number of chromosomes as female bees. A male passes on an exact copy of his chromosomes to his daughters, while the female queen only passes on half of hers.

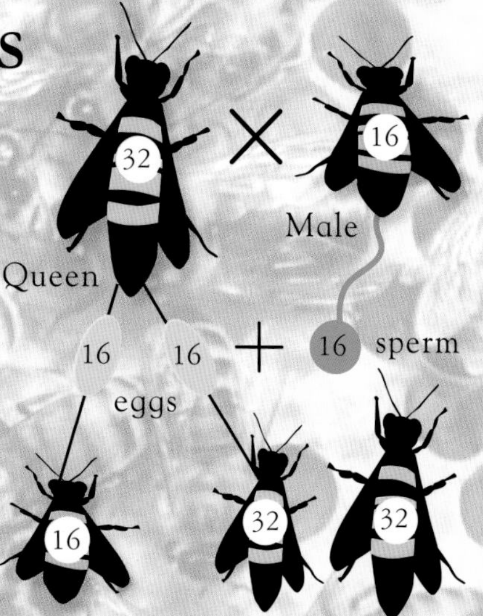

This means that the workers that have the same father are super sisters, sharing 75% of their genes (which is more than if they had their own offspring). So, by raising their larval super sisters to reach adulthood, the workers are ensuring that more of their genes are carried in the hive.

the colony or for their own benefit?

Playing God

We can now do a great deal to *alter* not only our OWN GENES but also those of every other animal and plant. But our ability to *manipulate* genes can have positive and *negative* effects. Just because we can do something, DOESN'T ALWAYS MEAN WE SHOULD.

Biodiversity

As in all debates, there are *pros* and *cons* to be considered.

The number of species on this planet and the way they interact are important in maintaining the health and survival of all organisms. However, human activity is driving many species to extinction. This loss of species could have disastrous consequences. When a colony dies, its genes go with it. If the gene pool shrinks, variation decreases and can limit the ability of an organism to adapt to change. This leaves any remaining members of the species vulnerable to a sudden change in their environment. If this species is a key link in a food chain, it may also affect organisms that depend on it.

EXTINCT

EXTINCT

EXTINCT

Reduced biodiversity MAY result in

Food crops

Scientists are trying to develop *crops* with improved characteristics using biotechnology. *Their main goals* are to help crops grow in *difficult environments*, improve their nutritional value, and make them more resistant to pests. *Opponents* of these crops argue that bioengineered genes *might escape* into the environment and could affect *wild* varieties, and may also have unknown consequences on *humans* and animals eating them.

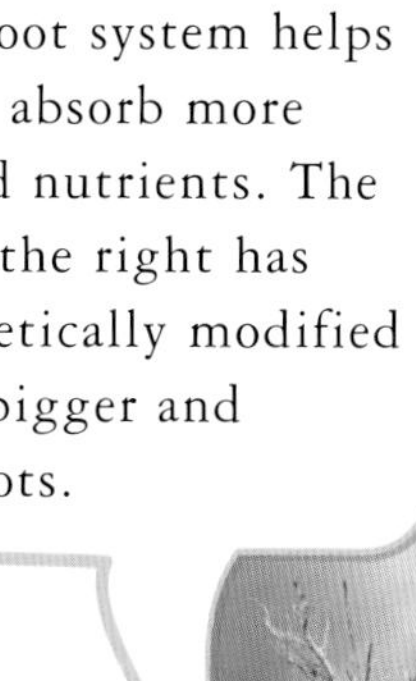

A large root system helps plants to absorb more water and nutrients. The plant on the right has been genetically modified to grow bigger and better roots.

Designer babies

Advances in science mean that not only can people who were unable to have children now have them, but in some cases they can choose for their baby to have certain traits. This is useful if there is a genetic disease in the family that is only carried by or affects one sex. But while many people think this is an acceptable use of gene technology, scientists are coming under pressure to select for other traits, such as hair or eye color. The ethics of whether this is a desirable thing to do are only just starting to be debated.

Cloning

Cloning is the technique of taking a cell from an animal or plant, extracting its DNA, and inserting it into another cell to create an exact copy of the original organism. Those in favor of cloning point to its benefits in spreading superior genes over larger populations of animals and plants rather than waiting for the results of crossbreeding. Those against it point to the unknown effects of these genes on the health and biodiversity of species.

*the **loss** of potentially **useful** genes.*

Jurassic Park

Could we bring back the dinosaurs? They did it in the movies, but is it technically possible? And do we *really* want to?

Back to the bird

Re-creating an extinct animal is much harder in real life than it is in the movies. Scientists face a number of *problems*, the main one being that DNA, an animal's genetic code, does not survive for long once the animal is dead. **Most fossils**, including those of the dinosaurs, *are too old to recover any DNA*. One way around the problem would be to start with an existing animal and work backward. We know that birds are descended from the dinosaurs, so it may be possible to RE-CREATE A DINO by switching genes on or off in birds. Scientists have already managed to make bird embryos grow longer tails and feathers on their scaly legs.

GRRR!!

But what would we do with a ***DINOSAUR*** *even if we did manage to grow a new one?*

THE BIGGEST BIRD EGG YOU COULD USE TO MAKE A DINOSAUR IS THAT OF AN OSTRICH. THIS COULD GROW A DINO THE SIZE OF A VELOCIRAPTOR.

Tyrannosaurus rex was one of the most fearsome predators that ever lived.

Rare as hen's teeth

Birds have not had teeth for 70 million years, but researchers have found them in the embryos of mutant chickens. It is thought birds lost their teeth to grow beaks instead, but still have the potential to make them. The teeth were just like those of a crocodile—another relative of the dinosaur.

Teeth forming in the beak of a chicken

In the film *Jurassic Park*, scientists extracted dinosaur DNA from **BLOOD** in the gut of an insect **trapped in amber**. Scientists have attempted to do this in *real life*, but with little success. Instead, they found that these insects **CARRIED DISEASES** that could have helped to **kill off** the dinosaurs.

Making the switch

Scientists have taken DNA from an extinct Tasmanian tiger and planted it into a mouse embryo to see what would happen. They found that the DNA switches on a gene that makes cartilage that later becomes the mouse's limb and tail bones. Even though it won't bring back the Tasmanian tiger, this shows that extinct genes can be made to work again.

Mammoth task

We probably have more chance of re-creating mammoths than bringing back dinosaurs. They only became extinct around 10,000 years ago and some have been found frozen in ice. Ice preserves DNA, so it might be possible to take the eggs or sperm from frozen mammoths and implant them in an Asian elephant. This could give us an animal that is at least 50% mammoth.

I may not look scary but I have great potential!

Archaeopteryx, one of the first birds, had teeth, claws on its wings, and a long tail.

From wings to forelimbs

You can't usually see the fingers in a bird's wing, but they sometimes appear as claws in baby birds, such as moorhens or hoatzins. Since the genes are already there, it may be possible to transform a bird's wings back into the front claws of a dinosaur.

Moorhen's wing claw

EVOLUTION IN ACTION

Many of Darwin's theories about evolution were based on his careful observations of how things looked and worked. However, many vital pieces of information were missing, and he could only hope that new discoveries would prove him right.

Today, scientists are beginning to fill in many of the gaps. New fossils have been found, and DNA technology is uncovering surprising connections between plant and animal species. Even so, there is still a long way to go in our understanding of evolution.

There remains one BIG question:
Are humans still evolving, or have we reached our limits?
We can only wait and see.

EARTH FORMS, VOLCANOES POUR GASES INTO THE SKY, AND WATER VAPOR RAINS DOWN TO FORM OCEANS. IT'S VERY HOT, AND THERE'S NO OXYGEN.

Story of life

Our planet is 4.5 billion years old. In its early days, Earth was a hot rock surrounded by poisonous gases. A cocktail of chemicals was washed into the oceans, where they reacted and formed molecules that began to copy themselves. Small changes in these molecules allowed better copiers, called nucleic acids, to dominate. This was the start of natural selection.

Underwater events

Some scientists think life may have begun around vents on the seabed. These vents blast out hot chemicals from the center of the Earth, and could have provided the energy for them to combine into bigger molecules.

The ability of molecules (groups of atoms) to join and copy themselves was a key step in the development of life.

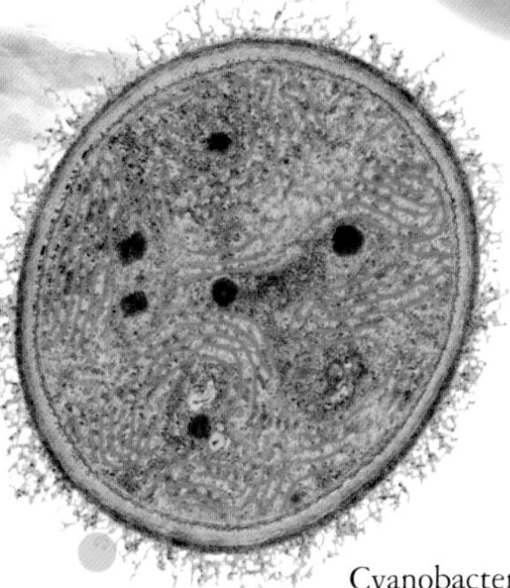

Cyanobacteria

Living stromatolites in Australia

3,800 MYA SIMPLE SINGLE-CELL BACTERIA APPEAR

CYANOBACTERIA OXYGENATE EARTH'S POISONOUS OCEANS

3,200 MYA ATMOSPHERIC OXYGEN INCREASES

4,000 3,600 million years ago (mya) 3,200 mya

Cells

Once an efficient copying mechanism had developed into the complex chemical DNA, the next step was to enclose it in a membrane that would protect it from the external environment. These simple organisms were prototypes of the first bacteria.

Stepping up the gas

The appearance of cyanobacteria (blue-green algae) was the first step toward making Earth's oceans inhabitable. These produced oxygen using photosynthesis, a process that uses sunlight to turn carbon dioxide and water into sugars and oxygen.

Stromatolites

Stromatolites are rock structures formed by mats of cyanobacteria. They released oxygen into the atmosphere, where it reacted with ultraviolet light to form a protective layer of ozone around Earth that shields life from harmful rays.

First animals

The first major evidence of multicellular animals is seen in the Ediacaran fossils of Canada. These are mainly soft-bodied, worm- or jellylike animals, but they show that many new body shapes had already evolved.

This fossil from the Precambrian period is thought to be an Ediacaran jellyfish.

I'M HALLUCIGENIA AND I'VE GOT LEGS, SPINES, AND A LONG GUT. IT'S A SPECIES-EAT-SPECIES WORLD OUT THERE!

Lichens are a combination of an alga and a fungus that live together.

Protists are single or multicelled organisms that have a nucleus. They are the ancestors of all plants, fungi, and animals.

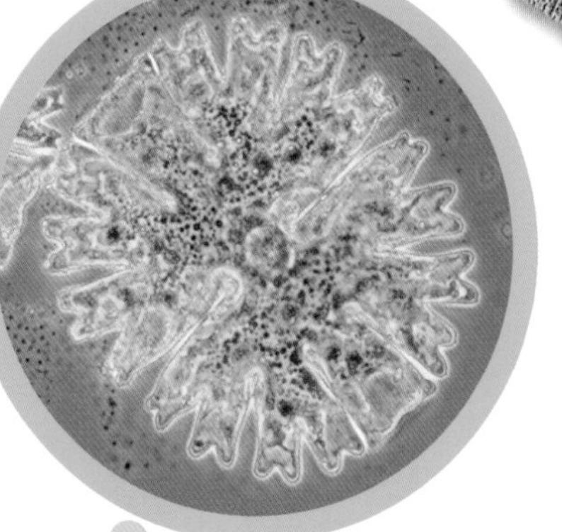

Lichens

Lichens were the first complex organisms to colonize the land. They absorbed large amounts of carbon dioxide from the atmosphere and replaced it with oxygen. As the carbon dioxide levels went down, the temperature cooled, which may have triggered a series of global ice ages. The increase in oxygen also allowed early animals to grow bigger and more complicated.

BOOM CAMBRIAN EXPLOSION

The sudden appearance of lots of new fossil species at the beginning of the Cambrian period puzzled Darwin. This explosion of life forms may have occurred after a rapid rise in oxygen levels or because a large number of new habitats became available.

1,800 MYA
FIRST COMPLEX LIFE FORMS (PROTISTS)

635 MYA
END OF LAST SNOWBALL EARTH

700 mya

630 mya

542

1,300 MYA
FIRST FUNGI

Snowball Earth

Earth turned into a giant snowball several times in its early history. Despite ice hundreds of yards thick, some algae, bacteria, and fungi managed to survive because they contained proteins that had evolved to work in the cold.

Snack attack

Many of the creatures that evolved in the early Cambrian have features that show animals had begun to eat each other. A single gummy bite may have been behind the evolution of teeth, feet, intestines, spines, and hard shells.

Cambrian period 542–488 mya

The Cambrian was when animal life forms really began to diversify. What little land there was above sea level lay clustered around the equator. Because the atmosphere still had little oxygen, everything lived in the sea. Sponges, worms, mollusks, and reef-building animals were abundant. Trilobites, a group of hard-shelled invertebrates, made their first appearance. Many of the Cambrian animals had weird shapes and features that are no longer seen. Land plants had not yet evolved.

TRILOBITES DOMINATED THE SEAS FOR 300 MILLION YEARS. THEY HAD UNIQUE EYES THAT ENABLED THEM TO SEE THEIR PREY.

Ordovician period 488–443 mya

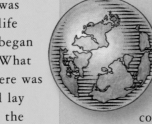

The continents had begun to move together by the beginning of the Ordovician and would end up covered in ice at the South Pole. The first corals appeared, along with snails, clams, and squidlike animals. Armored jawless fish swam among sea lilies growing up from the seafloor. A few arthropods began to take their first tentative steps on to the land.

SEA LILIES WERE ACTUALLY ANIMALS, RELATED TO MODERN STARFISH AND FEATHER STARS.

Silurian period 443–416 mya

The melting of the ice that had formed at the end of the Ordovician caused a huge rise in sea level. Many species had died out, creating opportunities for others to take over. The numbers of jawless fish increased and they began to colonize freshwater rivers. At the same time, fish with jaws appeared. Giant scorpions roamed the seabed and corals formed large reefs. The first plants began to colonize the land.

THE FIRST **LAND PLANTS** LOOKED VERY LIKE MODERN WHISK FERNS, WHICH HAVE SIMPLE ROOTS.

542mya

488mya

443mya

Brand **NEW** *shell* suit

BRACHIOPODS (LAMPSHELLS) WERE COMMON ON THE CAMBRIAN SEAFLOOR. THEY STILL EXIST TODAY, BUT THERE ARE FEWER SPECIES.

Cothurnocystis elizae

THIS **STRANGE** CREATURE IS THOUGHT TO BE THE **ANCESTOR** OF **ALL** ANIMALS WITH A BACKBONE, INCLUDING HUMANS.

THE FIRST FISH HAD **NO JAWS**. IN SOME, THE HEAD WAS COVERED BY A **BONY PLATE** THAT ACTED LIKE A **SHIELD**. THEY ALSO HAD AN INTERNAL SKELETON TO SUPPORT THE MUSCLES.

Devonian period 416–359 mya

Life in the water was dominated by fish—primitive sharks began to increase in number and the first bony and lobe-finned fish appeared. Ammonites were the latest mollusks to arrive and trilobites began to decline. By the end of the period the lobe-finned fish had begun to walk on their fins and haul themselves on to the land as the first tetrapods. Plants were diverging rapidly on land, providing homes for wingless insects.

One *small* step for a **TETRAPOD**, one giant leap for evolution.

Carboniferous period 359–299 mya

Large primitive trees now dominated coastal swamps and formed huge forests. Tetrapods started to walk on land and evolve into amphibians. Insects grew wings and took to the air. Marine life flourished—mollusks, corals, and crinoids were abundant. Sharks were also common and diverse. At the end of the period the first reptiles emerged from eggs that could be laid on land.

A fossil tree trunk

EVER WONDERED WHERE COAL COMES FROM? SWAMPS WERE IDEAL FOR PRESERVING THE TRUNKS OF MILLIONS OF TREES. DEAD TRUNKS WERE COVERED IN MUD AND PRESSED TO FORM COAL SEAMS.

Permian period 299–251 mya

All the continents joined together to form the supercontinent Pangaea. This reduced the length of coastline and many marine animals became extinct. The interior became a massive desert. The first seed plants (conifers) and mosses appeared. Amphibians and reptiles began to diversify, including groups that would go on to become dinosaurs and mammals.

DIMETRODON WAS A MAMMAL-LIKE REPTILE WITH SPECIAL TEETH FOR EATING MEAT.

416 mya — 359 mya — 299 mya

A breath of fresh air...

LUNGFISH WERE A TYPE OF LOBE-FINNED FISH THAT EVOLVED A **LUNG** AS WELL AS GILLS TO HELP THEM GULP AIR FROM THE SURFACE.

Now try this!

Find out about the rocks in your area and the geological time periods they belong to (the local library or museum should be able to help). Then collect pictures of fossils that have been found in these rocks and make a map of what was living in your neighborhood millions of years ago.

COELACANTHS WERE A GROUP OF FISH THAT WERE THOUGHT TO HAVE BECOME EXTINCT AT THE END OF THE CRETACEOUS, UNTIL ONE WAS CAUGHT IN 1938.

Triassic
period 251–199 mya

The warm and dry conditions of the Triassic were ideal for reptiles to flourish on land. They also flew in the sky (pterosaurs) and swam in the sea (ichthyosaurs). Early crocodiles and turtles inhabited riverbanks. In the sea, ammonites were abundant and the first starfish and sea urchins appeared. Conifers, gingkos, cycads, and seed ferns took over from coal-forming trees, and the first flowering plants sprouted. Small nocturnal mammals survived the extinction that marked the end of the period.

MODERN **MAGNOLIAS** (RIGHT) HAVE CHANGED VERY LITTLE SINCE THEY FIRST EVOLVED (LEFT).

Jurassic
period 199–145 mya

The Jurassic is famous as the age of the dinosaurs. Huge sauropods ate cycads and ferns and were preyed on by meat-eating allosaurs and megalosaurs. The first birds evolved from small, feathery dinosaurs. Modern sharks appeared and amphibians began to look more like modern frogs and toads. Pangaea began to split apart, flooding large areas of land.

EARLY **BIRDS** STILL LOOKED LIKE THEIR **DINOSAUR** ANCESTORS, WITH **TEETH** AND **WING CLAWS.**

Cretaceous
period 145–65 mya

The modern continents began to take shape. This was the time of the giant dinosaurs, particularly meat eaters such as *Tyrannosaurus rex*. Flowering plants started to spread and insects diversified to pollinate them. Birds pushed the pterosaurs to extinction. New mammals emerged, including the ancestors of the marsupials.

RUN *boys!*

251 mya **199** mya **145** mya

THE **ICHTHYOSAUR**, A DOLPHINLIKE REPTILE, SWAM IN **TRIASSIC** SEAS.

SAUROPODS SUCH AS THE **BRACHIOSAURUS** WERE LARGE, PLANT-EATING DINOSAURS.

Megazostrodon

Megazostrodon was a tiny shrewlike mammal. Its hair kept it warm while it searched for food at night. It laid eggs and looked after its young.

Mass extinction

The end of the Cretaceous is marked by the extinction of a large number of species, including the dinosaurs. No one is sure what happened, but many think Earth was hit by an asteroid. This threw up clouds of dust that changed the climate and disrupted food chains. The survivors were those that could adapt to new conditions.

Tertiary

period 65–1.8 mya

Mammals took over the role of the largest life forms and diversified to fill habitats left by reptiles and dinosaurs. Most of the modern forms of fish, invertebrates, birds, insects, and flowering plants evolved during this period. The first hominins (early forms of humans) appeared at the end of the period. The climate began to cool dramatically, favoring the rise of grasslands and grazing animals.

AT 20 FT (6 M) TALL, **GIANT SLOTHS** WERE TOO BIG TO HANG AROUND IN TREES.

Quaternary

period 1.8 mya to present

This period started with an ice age. The continents had reached their current positions but a number of land bridges allowed species to cross continents. Giant mammals, such as mammoths, had adapted to the cold but began to die out as the climate warmed. Hunting by humans may have speeded up the process. Large carnivores, such as saber-toothed cats and cave bears, also vanished. Many species of humans evolved and died out, leaving *Homo sapiens* as the sole survivor.

SABER-TOOTHED CATS WERE THE MOST **FEROCIOUS** PREDATORS OF THEIR DAY.

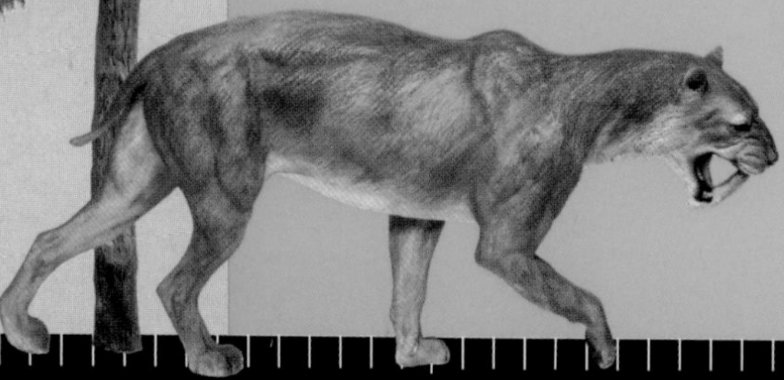

TYRANNOSAURUS REX

65 mya

1.8 mya

OUR EARLIEST **ANCESTORS** APPEARED ABOUT 5 MILLION YEARS AGO.

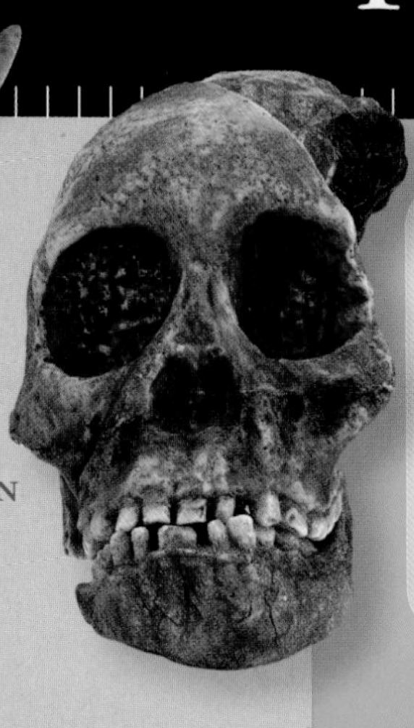

And here we are

Modern man, *Homo sapiens*, emerged 250,000 years ago. Until 25,000 years ago we lived alongside the Neanderthals, who were stronger and more stockily built. It is not clear what happened to them.

Missing links

One of the biggest problems Darwin faced in his theory of evolution were gaps in the fossil record that showed evolutionary changes. Geology was a new science at the time and dating rocks and fossils was difficult. Since then, many new discoveries have been made that are helping to fill in the gaps.

Written in stone

This page from an 1880 book shows how naturalists and geologists attempted to match the fossils they had found to the sequence of rocks in their area.

From scales to feathers

One of the first "missing links" to be found was *Archaeopteryx*, a winged fossil that showed a change, or transition, from a dinosaur to a bird. A number of other fossils have since been found, including a nonflying dromaeosaur that had downy feathers from head to tail, suggesting feathers may first have evolved as a way to keep warm.

Fishapods

Tiktaalik, a transitional form between a fish and a walking tetrapod, shows how this "fishapod" had developed wrist and finger bones that enabled it to prop itself up on its fins. Holes on top of its head suggest it may have breathed air through primitive lungs.

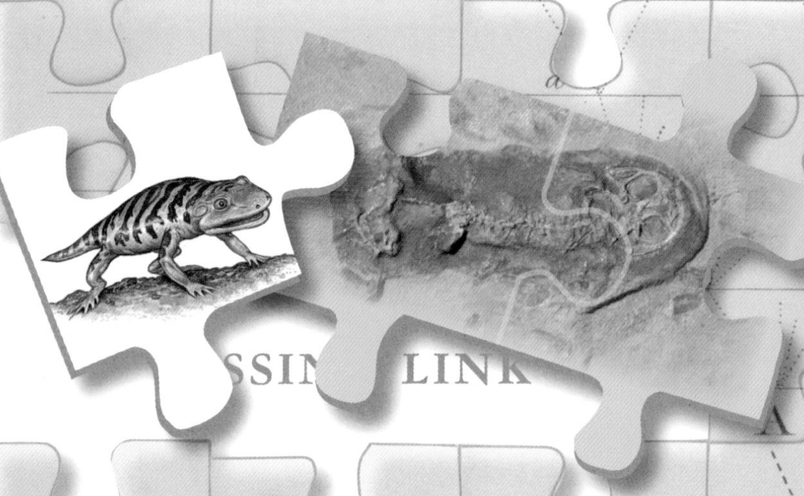

Frogs and salamanders

An ancestor of frogs and salamanders that shows features of both was identified in 2008. *Gerobatrachus hottoni* is like a salamander in shape but has a froglike head and jaw. Frogs and salamanders are now thought to have split into separate species between 240 and 275 million years ago.

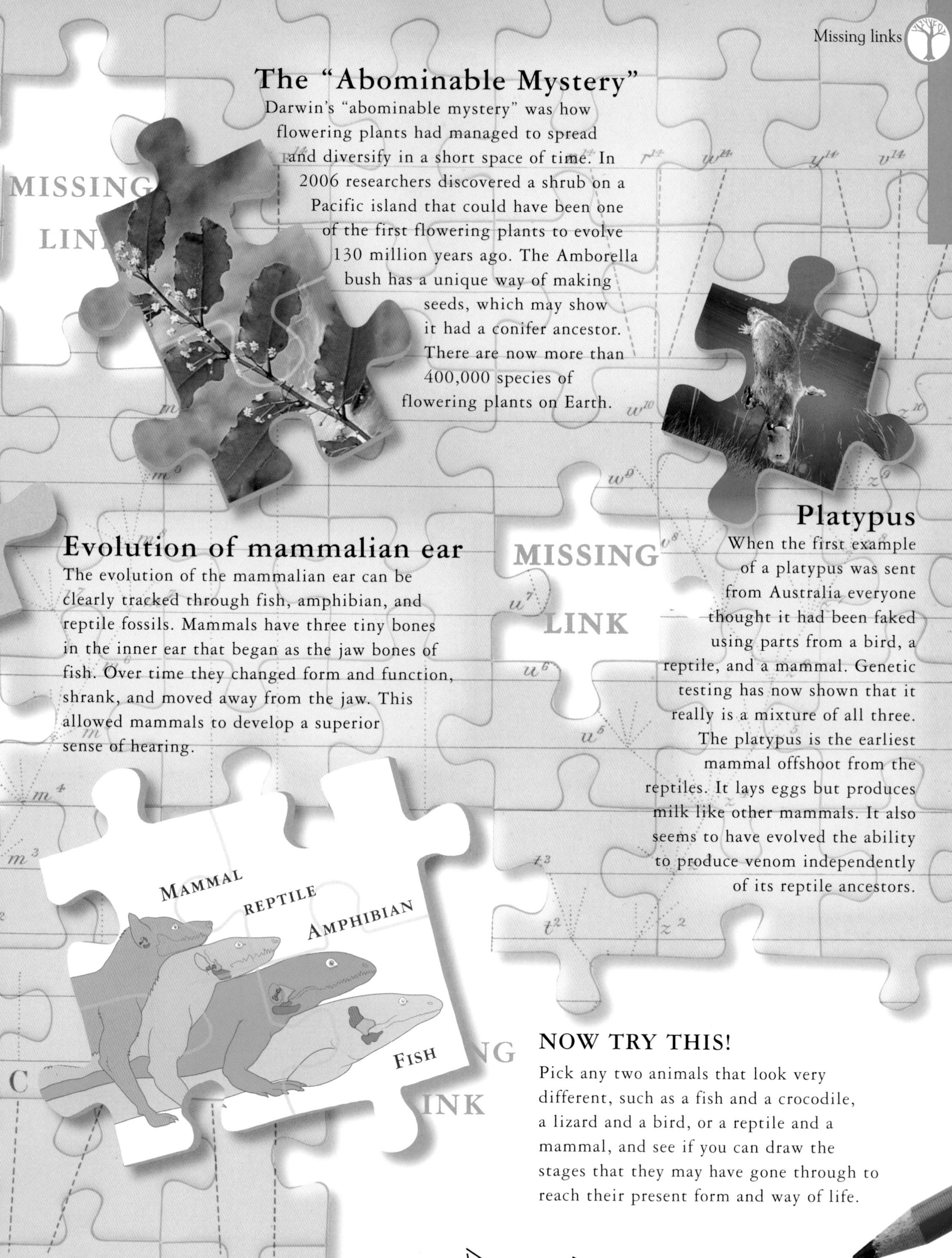

The "Abominable Mystery"

Darwin's "abominable mystery" was how flowering plants had managed to spread and diversify in a short space of time. In 2006 researchers discovered a shrub on a Pacific island that could have been one of the first flowering plants to evolve 130 million years ago. The Amborella bush has a unique way of making seeds, which may show it had a conifer ancestor. There are now more than 400,000 species of flowering plants on Earth.

Evolution of mammalian ear

The evolution of the mammalian ear can be clearly tracked through fish, amphibian, and reptile fossils. Mammals have three tiny bones in the inner ear that began as the jaw bones of fish. Over time they changed form and function, shrank, and moved away from the jaw. This allowed mammals to develop a superior sense of hearing.

Platypus

When the first example of a platypus was sent from Australia everyone thought it had been faked using parts from a bird, a reptile, and a mammal. Genetic testing has now shown that it really is a mixture of all three. The platypus is the earliest mammal offshoot from the reptiles. It lays eggs but produces milk like other mammals. It also seems to have evolved the ability to produce venom independently of its reptile ancestors.

NOW TRY THIS!

Pick any two animals that look very different, such as a fish and a crocodile, a lizard and a bird, or a reptile and a mammal, and see if you can draw the stages that they may have gone through to reach their present form and way of life.

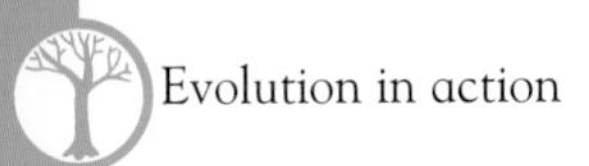

Islands apart

Many islands have plants and animals that do not live anywhere else. Their ancestors were on the island when it broke away from the mainland or have swum, flown, or been carried on rafts to the island since. Once on the island, the animals and plants adapted to fill new or vacant niches.

Madagascar

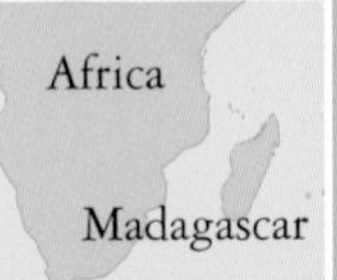

Madagascar is one of the most biodiverse islands on Earth. It split from Africa 165 million years ago. This was long before any of Africa's large mammals, such as elephants and giraffes had evolved, which is why they do not live there.

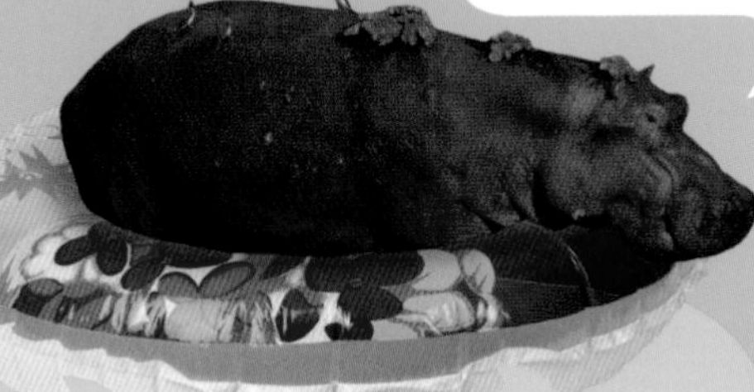

Good thing I brought my rubber ring!

Hippos are thought to be the only large mammals to have swum to Madagascar.

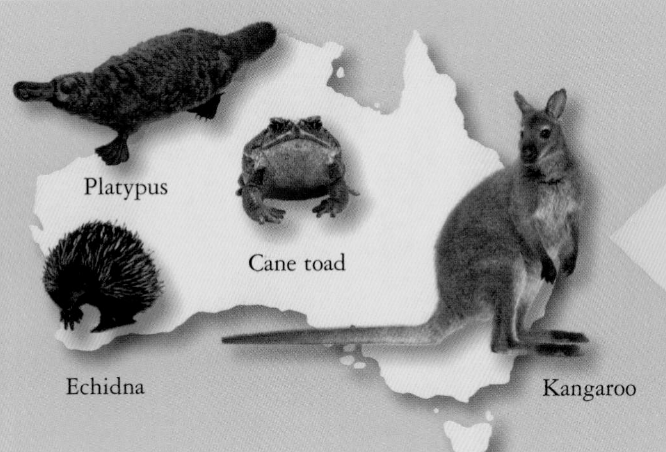

Australia

This is home to two groups of special mammals. The monotremes comprise the echidnas and the platypus, and the marsupials include kangaroos, koalas, possums, bandicoots, and wombats.

The Galápagos

South America
Galápagos
My ambition is to be big in the Galápagos.

Galápagos tortoises have grown huge because they have no predators.

These are a group of volcanic islands in the Pacific. They were never attached to the mainland, so all the species on them have arrived from somewhere else. Even though these islands have similar animals and plants, many have adapted to suit the local environment and are different from those on other islands. This is shown by differences in the beaks of finches and the shells and sizes of tortoises.

Sometimes evolution on islands is not all one way. Researchers in the Caribbean have found that Anolis lizards are washed into the sea during hurricanes and end up on a new island, where they breed with the local species. This mixes up the gene pool and slows down evolution. Other island animals, usually birds and bats, have returned to the mainland and evolved to suit their new home.

Anolis lizard

Madagascar is famous for its unique animals. These include primates (lemurs, sifakas, and aye-ayes), tenrecs, and chameleons. Since the island has been occupied by humans, many of the larger animals, such as the giant lemur, giant tortoises, pygmy hippo, and elephant bird, have died out. The rest are threatened by loss of habitat.

Ring-tailed lemur

Tenrec

Jackson's chameleon

Oi! Oz is over here, mate!

Although Australia is an island it is very close to the islands of Indonesia, which has allowed people and animals to cross. In some cases, the native animals and plants that had evolved to suit the local habitat have faced competition from invading species. The dingo replaced the Tasmanian tiger, which was hunted to extinction by humans, as the largest carnivore. Cane toads were introduced as a form of pest control in fields of sugar cane but are now pests themselves because they have no natural predators.

Dingo

No way. I want to be in Amer-i-ca, plenty of trees in Amer-i-ca...

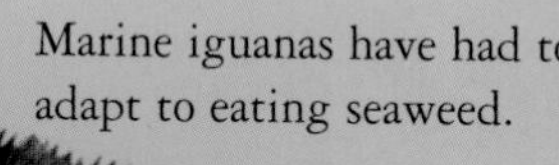

Some possums crossed to the New World before the continents split.

Finches on the Galápagos have evolved different beaks that suit the type of food available on each island.

The Galápagos Islands

I'm only here for the sun, the sea, and the seaweed.

Marine iguanas have had to adapt to eating seaweed.

Same, *but different*

All life forms develop characteristics that suit where they live, what they eat, or how they move. This often results in species that look similar even though they are ***not related***. Take these five animals, for example...

armadillos *in N. America,*
anteaters *in S. America,*
aardvarks *and...*
What are the ants like in your part of the world?
Well, they're sort of tickly...

Bats and birds both fly, *but their wings*

Bats use a fast rowing motion to fly.

It's really difficult to scratch that itch with these fingers.

Thumb

Wrist bones

Fingers

It's a wing thing

It may have wings, but is it a bird? No—it could be a bat or an insect. Just because two animals have the same feature it doesn't mean they have a common ancestor. Sometimes things look the same because they have the same function. Birds and bats do not have a common winged ancestor so their wings show big differences.

Bats

Looking at this skeleton of a bat you can see its arm bones are very like those of a human. But instead of our own dainty digits it has oversized fingers that it uses to support the tough skin of the wing. Bats change the shape of their wings by flexing their fingers, which makes it easy for them to maneuver.

SIMILARITIES

- A flexible nose helps them root out insects.
- They have long, sticky tongues that trap ants and termites. Anteaters can flick their tongues in and out 150 times a minute.
- They produce lots of saliva to keep the tongue sticky.
- All have strong claws for digging out ant hills.
- Aardvarks and armadillos have a few peg teeth; the rest have none.

pangolins in Africa, and echidnas in Australia.

are not the same.

Large birds find it easier to glide than to keep flapping their wings.

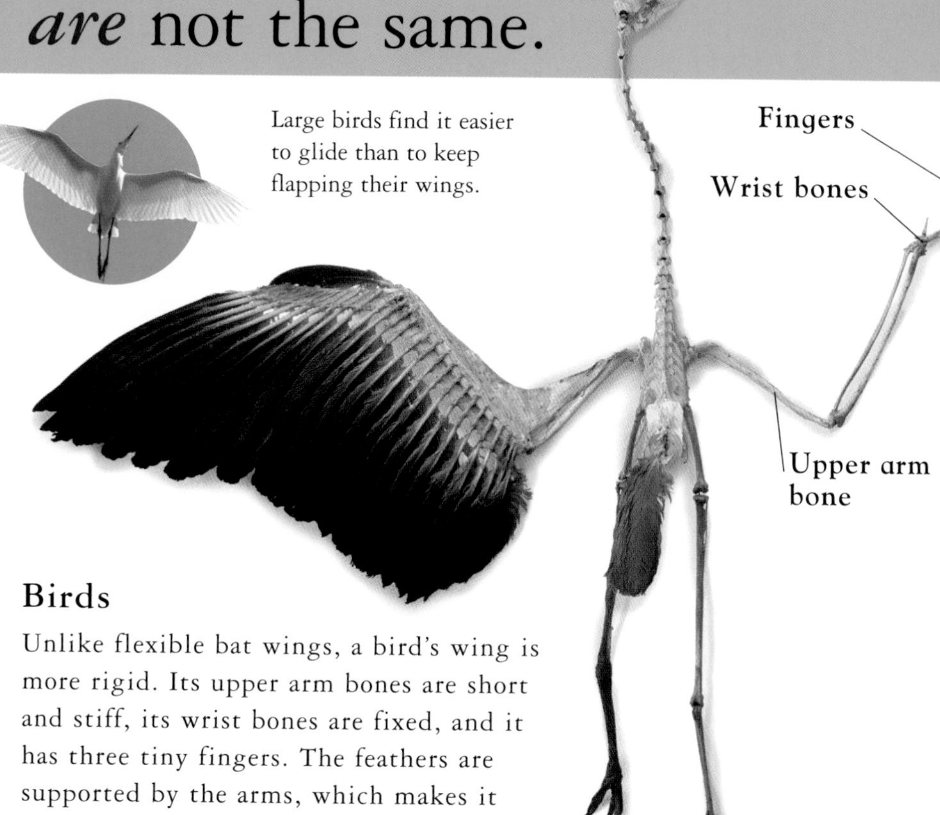

Birds

Unlike flexible bat wings, a bird's wing is more rigid. Its upper arm bones are short and stiff, its wrist bones are fixed, and it has three tiny fingers. The feathers are supported by the arms, which makes it difficult to change direction quickly.

Parallel lines

When unrelated species develop along similar lines to fill the same role in their environment it is called convergent evolution. Related species, such as porcupines in the Americas and Africa, can also develop the same characteristics (in this case, quills) at the same time even though they have been physically separated for thousands of years. This process is sometimes called parallel evolution.

Poison dart frog

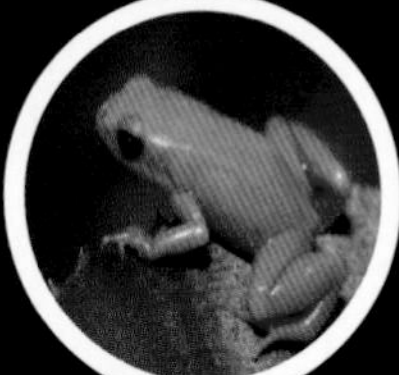

Mantella

Beware of the frog

South American poison dart frogs and the unrelated mantella frog of Madagascar have both developed a mechanism for storing poison from the ants that they eat in their skins. They have also developed bright skin colors as a warning.

Koala

Human

Finger of suspicion

Koalas are one of the few non-primates that have developed fingerprints. They are almost identical to human fingerprints, and each koala's prints are different. However, its closest relative, the wombat, doesn't have prints. Finger ridges help animals to grip things.

EmbryOs

EMBRYO: the early stage of an animal before it is born or hatches.

The embryos of many animals look very similar in the early stages of development. Some features will continue growing to become limbs, teeth, or tails; others will vanish before the animal is born.

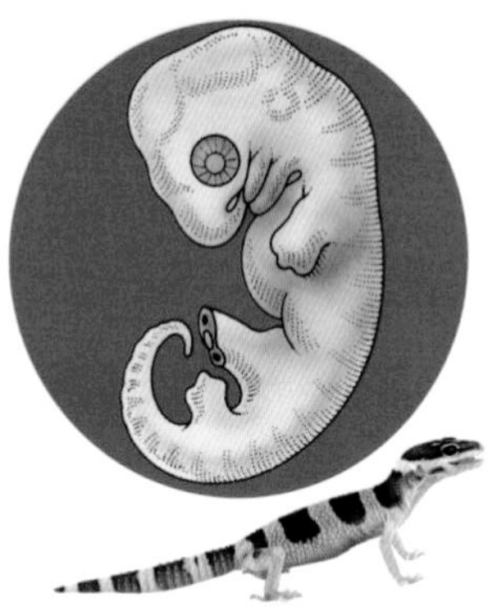

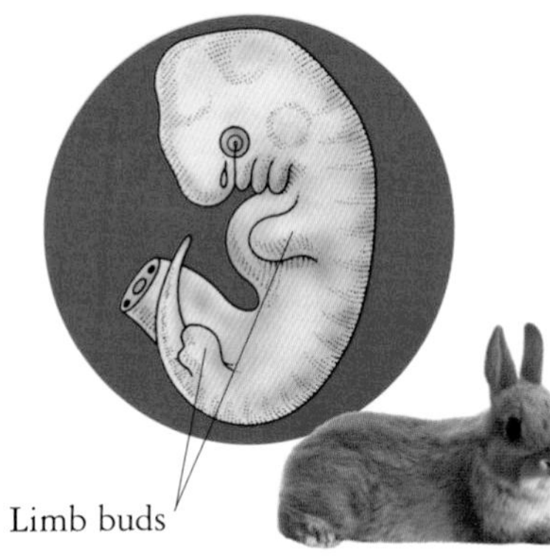

Limb buds

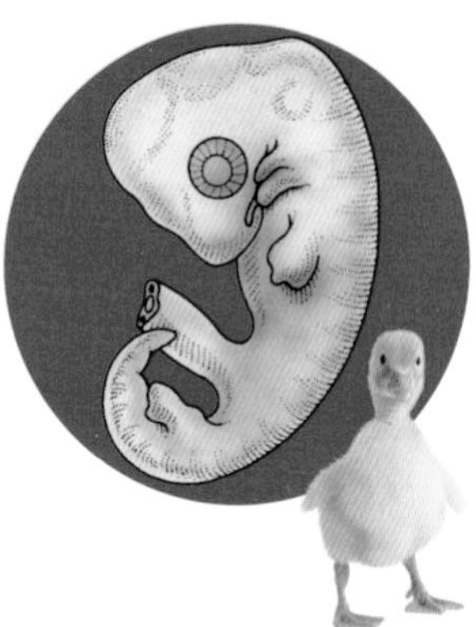

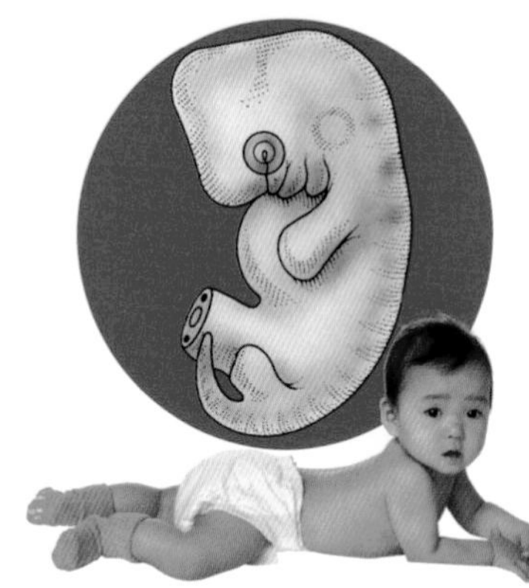

Spot the difference

Generally, embryos develop in an order that follows when each structure first evolved. The backbone is one of the earliest features to form in all vertebrates, with a head at one end and a tail at the other. Four limb buds then appear, as do the eyes. In the weeks that follow, the embryos become less alike as genes turn some things off and turn others on.

WHERE DID THAT COME FROM?

Every now and then an animal is born with an organ or structure that was common in one of its distant ancestors. Although it is of no use to the modern animal, its reappearance gives an indication of how genetic changes lead to new species.

On their toes

Modern horses have only one toe but their earliest ancestors had as many as five. Sometimes a foal is born with two tiny toes either side of the main hoof toe.

Tall tales

Stories of human babies being born with a short tail may seem unbelievable, but it happens. All humans have genes to grow tails but they usually get switched off early in development.

Claws on paws

Dogs have four toes on each foot. Sometimes an extra "dew" claw forms higher up on the back or front legs. They are often removed to prevent injury while exercising.

Flippin' amazing

Inside some whales and dolphins are small bones that show they once had back legs and that their ancestors walked on land. These occasionally reappear as tiny rear flippers.

Just when you think you don't need

Ernst Haeckel

Haeckel was a German biologist who drew a series of embryos in various stages of development to go with his theory that an animal embryo passes through stages resembling its adult evolutionary ancestors. It was later proved that embryos look like other closely related species rather than their ancestors.

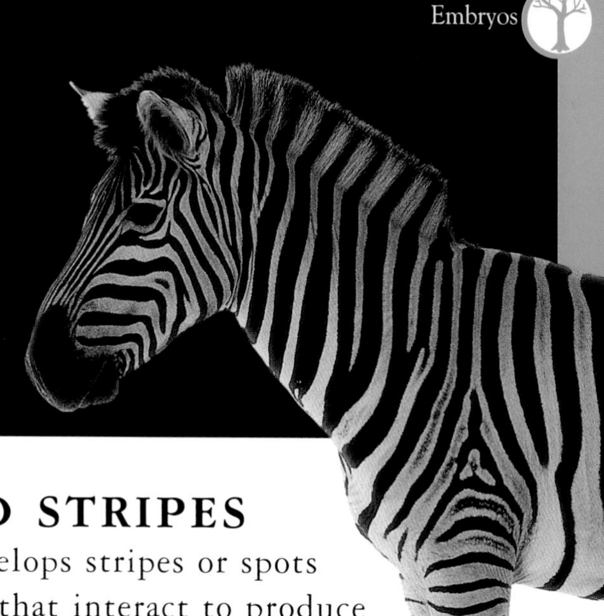

Spots and stripes

Whether an animal develops stripes or spots depends on two chemicals that interact to produce a pattern of spots in the skin of the embryo. These chemicals turn skin color on or off and determine how big the spots will be. If there is too much of one of the chemicals the spots join up to form stripes. The size of the animal is also crucial—very small animals, such as mice, have no spots. In most large animals, such as elephants, the spots are very small and all blend together.

Spots form before stripes. So, spotted animals can have striped tails, but striped animals cannot have spotted tails because their spots have already spread into stripes.

Hanging around

Many modern organisms have structures that had a practical use in their ancestors. Sometimes these have undergone a change of purpose, but more often they have become useless or have reached a point where they have only a limited function.

In a flap

Ostriches and emus have stumpy wings that can no longer be used to fly. Instead, the birds use them to balance themselves while running. They also flap them around in courtship displays.

Powerless flowers

Dandelions produce flowers and pollen, but neither of these is needed to produce seeds. The plant self-fertilizes to form seeds that will grow into clones of the parent plant.

Feeling their way

Moles and cave salamanders have eyes but do not use them. They have spent so long living in the dark that their eyes are useless for seeing anything other than light or shadow.

Hidden wings

Many species of earwigs have a pair of hindwings folded underneath leathery forewings. Earwigs rarely fly anywhere, even though they can—it takes them too long to unpack their wings.

something any more, it comes back!

Can *you* guess which of these are

We know that *humans* are related to **CHIMPS** and other members of the **ape family**. If we go back even further, we find we share ancestors with fish, *reptiles*, and insects. Ultimately, ***every living thing*** can trace

ANSWERS

A hippo (1) is the whale's (2) closest living relative. Whales once had four legs and walked on land.

Bears (3), seals (4), and dogs (5) are closely related carnivores but are on a different branch of the evolutionary tree from cats and hyenas.

Some snakes (6) have hip bones, which shows they once had four legs like lizards (7), their close cousins.

Birds (10) evolved from dinosaurs (8), and both are descended from reptiles. The closest living reptilian relation of a bird is the crocodile (9).

CLOSE RELATIVES?

its ancestry to a **bacteria** that lived *billions of years ago*. Sometimes it's easy to spot family connections, but the LINKS AREN'T ALWAYS OBVIOUS. See if you can figure out which of these are *close relatives*.

11 Cactus

12 Euphorbia

13 Spider crab

14 Horseshoe crab

15 Spider

16 Elephant

17 Dugong

18 Hyrax

19 Hoverfly

20 Wasp

21 Bumblebee

ANSWERS

Cacti (11) and euphorbias (12) are both desert plants but they are not related. They are an example of convergent evolution (see pages 76–77).

Horseshoe crabs (14) are not really crabs and are more closely related to spiders (15) than to spider crabs (13).

Dugongs (17) are the closest living relatives of the elephant (16) and they are both related to the hyrax (18).

Wasps (20) and bumblebees (21) are close relatives, but hoverflies (19) are not. They have evolved to look like wasps to deter predators.

Family trees

The horse family is often used as a classic example of how evolution works. There are plenty of horse fossils that show how minor changes occurred over millions of years. Some horses grew tall and then got smaller again, others kept three toes, while some rapidly diversified and equally quickly died out. They also show that many species of horse with different characteristics existed at the same time.

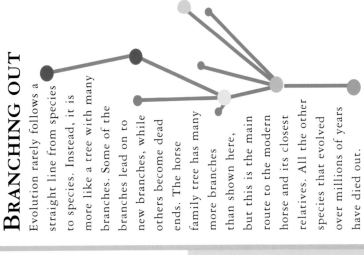

Branching out

Evolution rarely follows a straight line from species to species. Instead, it is more like a tree with many branches. Some of the branches lead on to new branches, while others become dead ends. The horse family tree has many more branches than shown here, but this is the main route to the modern horse and its closest relatives. All the other species that evolved over millions of years have died out.

Recent
2.6 MYA–PRESENT

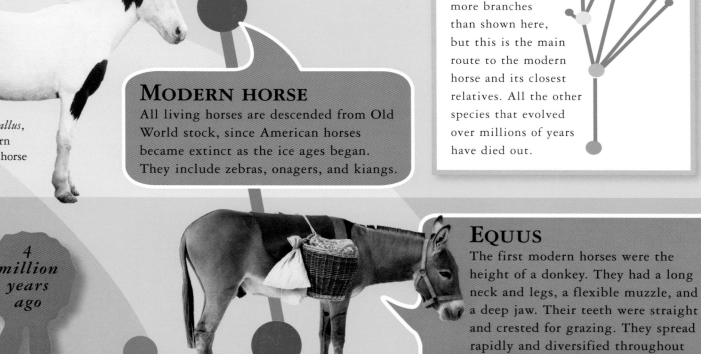

Equus caballus, the modern domestic horse

Modern horse

All living horses are descended from Old World stock, since American horses became extinct as the ice ages began. They include zebras, onagers, and kiangs.

Pliocene
5.3–2.6 MYA

One-toed hoof

4 million years ago

Equus

The first modern horses were the height of a donkey. They had a long neck and legs, a flexible muzzle, and a deep jaw. Their teeth were straight and crested for grazing. They spread rapidly and diversified throughout the Old and New Worlds.

Eocene

55–34 MYA (MILLION YEARS AGO)

55 million years ago

All horses began as an animal with four front toes.

Oligocene

34–23 MYA

36 million years ago

Three toes touched the ground, but still had pads.

Miocene

23–5.3 MYA

17 million years ago

Foot becomes adapted for running on hard ground.

15 million years ago

Side bones reduce to leave a central hoof.

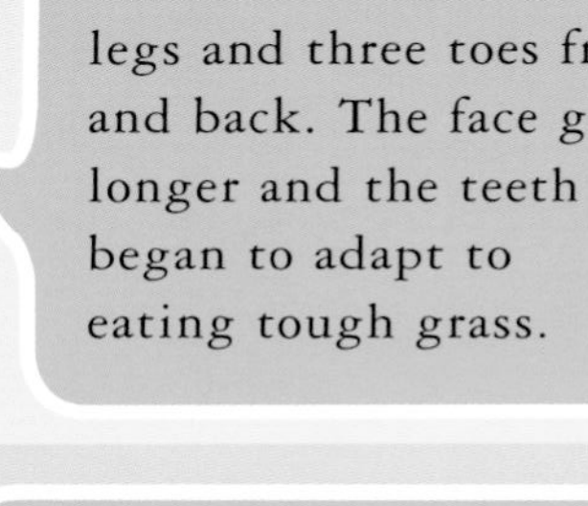

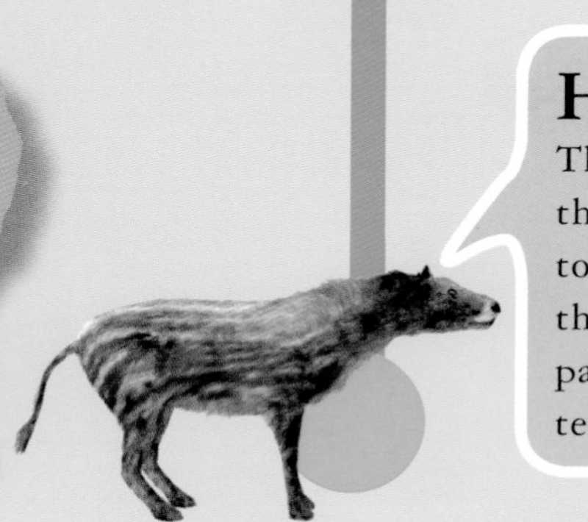

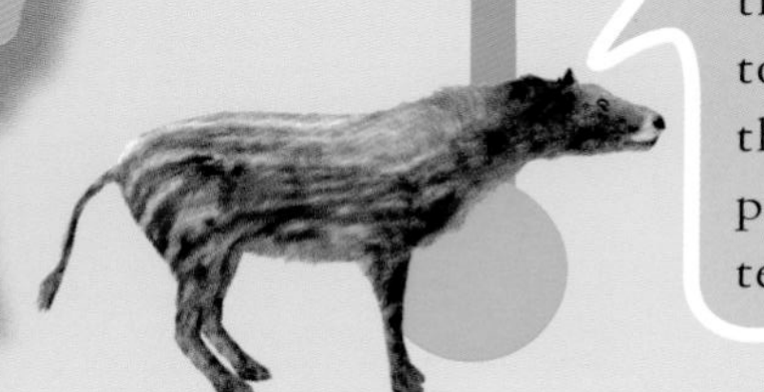

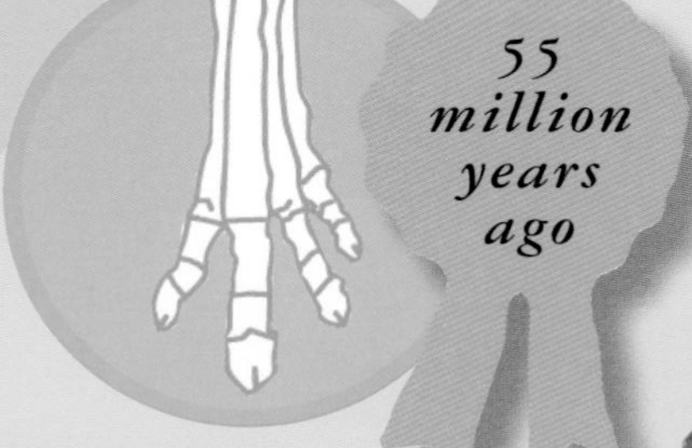

Pliohippus

This was once thought to be a direct ancestor of *Equus*. *Pliohippus* gradually lost its side toes and ran on a single hoof, but its teeth were curved and its face was different from modern horses.

Merychippus

These animals still had three toes but stood on tiptoe for faster running. The center toe was starting to develop into a hoof. The muzzle looked more horselike.

Miohippus

These horses had longer legs and three toes front and back. The face grew longer and the teeth began to adapt to eating tough grass.

Hyracotherium

The ancestor of the horse was the size of a dog. It had four toes on its front feet and three on the back, and had pads rather than hooves. Its teeth show it ate soft leaves.

Quagga returns

The quagga is a subspecies of the plains zebra that was wiped out in the 1870s. It differed from other zebras by having stripes only on its neck and head, while the rest of its body was brown. Using DNA from a stuffed quagga, scientists figured out its genetic code. Attempts are now being made to re-create it through selective breeding from existing zebras that have fewer stripes and brownish coats.

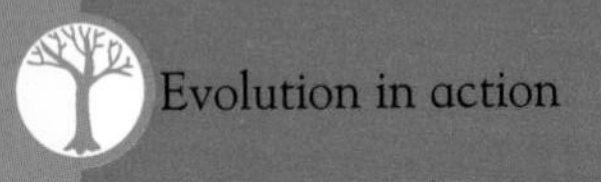

How the *elephant*

The elephant's trunk is an amazing example of evolutionary development. It is, in fact, a combined nose and upper lip that lengthened as the elephant's ancestors became taller and their tusks grew bigger. With such a heavy head, you need an easy way to touch the ground.

Can *your* nose do this?

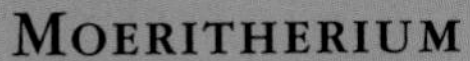

Moeritherium

This semiaquatic animal was small and had a long, mobile upper lip. It had enlarged incisor teeth, but these had not yet grown into tusks.

Paleomastodon

Paleomastodon is believed to be the first ancestor of the elephant line. *Moeritherium* and *Phiomia* are thought to be early side branches on the evolutionary tree.

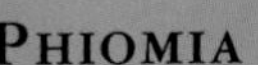

Phiomia

Phiomia had a short trunk formed from the nose and the upper lip. It also had short upper and lower tusks and a long bottom lip.

Gomphotherium

The gomphotheres had four tusks, the bottom two set into a shovel-like lower jaw. The trunk began to lengthen to help them feed and drink as the animals grew taller.

Primelephas

Primelephas was the ancestor of all modern elephants. It had smaller bottom tusks and a longer trunk than *Gomphotherium*.

Mastodons had cone-shaped teeth that were used to crush twigs and leaves from shrubs and trees. They lived near swamps and woodlands and may have used their tusks to knock over trees.

34 million years ago

23 million years ago

Eocene | **Oligocene** | **Miocene**

got his *trunk*

Asian elephants have only one lobe at the tip of their trunks so they have to wrap the trunk around objects to pick them up.

In Kipling's *Just So* story, the elephant went to the river for a drink. A crocodile grabbed his nose, which got longer and longer as he tried to pull free.

Mammoths were not as big as you might think—they were the same size as modern elephants, but had longer tusks and a high-domed head and shoulders.The trunk reached to the ground and had two flexible lobes at the end for grasping leaves.

ANANCUS

MAMMOTH

The teeth of mammoths and modern elephants evolved into a series of hard ridges that were better adapted to grinding up tough grasses.

Asian elephants are more closely related to mammoths than African elephants. They too have a slightly domed head but it is only the males that have tusks. The tip of an elephant's trunk is highly sensitive. It is not only used for breathing but also for sucking up water. The trunk can pick up objects and be waved aggressively.

ASIAN ELEPHANT

Mastodons were an early offshoot of the evolutionary tree. They had lost their lower tusks but the top ones were long and curved. They had a low-domed head and a shaggy coat.

MASTODON

STEGODON

AFRICAN ELEPHANT

African elephants have a flattened head and both sexes have tusks. Their trunks end in two lobes, which they can pinch together to pick up tiny objects.

5.3 million years ago

2.6 million years ago

10,000 years ago

Pliocene

Pleistocene

Today

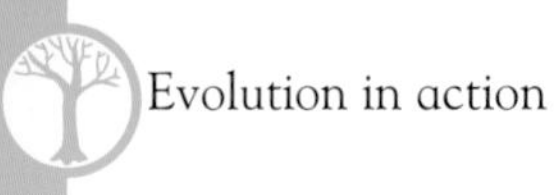

From ape *to human*

RELATIVE FACTS

Out of Africa

Darwin's idea that man was descended from the apes and came out of Africa upset many people. At that time there was little evidence—only a few Neanderthal skulls and bones had been found. Later, the bones of an early ape and the first example of *Homo erectus*, an early hominin from Java, were discovered. These were followed by examples of *Homo sapiens* dating back 30,000 years from Europe and Indonesia. It wasn't until 1967 that older fossils of *Homo sapiens* were discovered in Ethiopia. These have been dated back 195,000 years, proving that Darwin was correct.

Human evolution **is the most remarkable of any mammal.** No other species has developed as fast or colonized as much of the world as we have. Modern man, *Homo sapiens*, is the last of a series of humanlike creatures that we call hominins. Our early ancestors were small and apelike. They walked on two feet but bent their knees and hips. They ate leaves and fruit, but left the forest to search for other foods out on the savanna. As the diet changed, stronger teeth and jaws were required, which

It all began when I started walking upright and moved out of the forest...

I've gotten the hang of walking, but I still can't run. Physically, I'm taller and stronger, and I'm going places.

ARDIPITHECUS RAMIDUS

AUSTRALOPITHECUS (A.) ANAMENSIS

A. AFARENSIS

Human evolution has taken 5 million years. Many

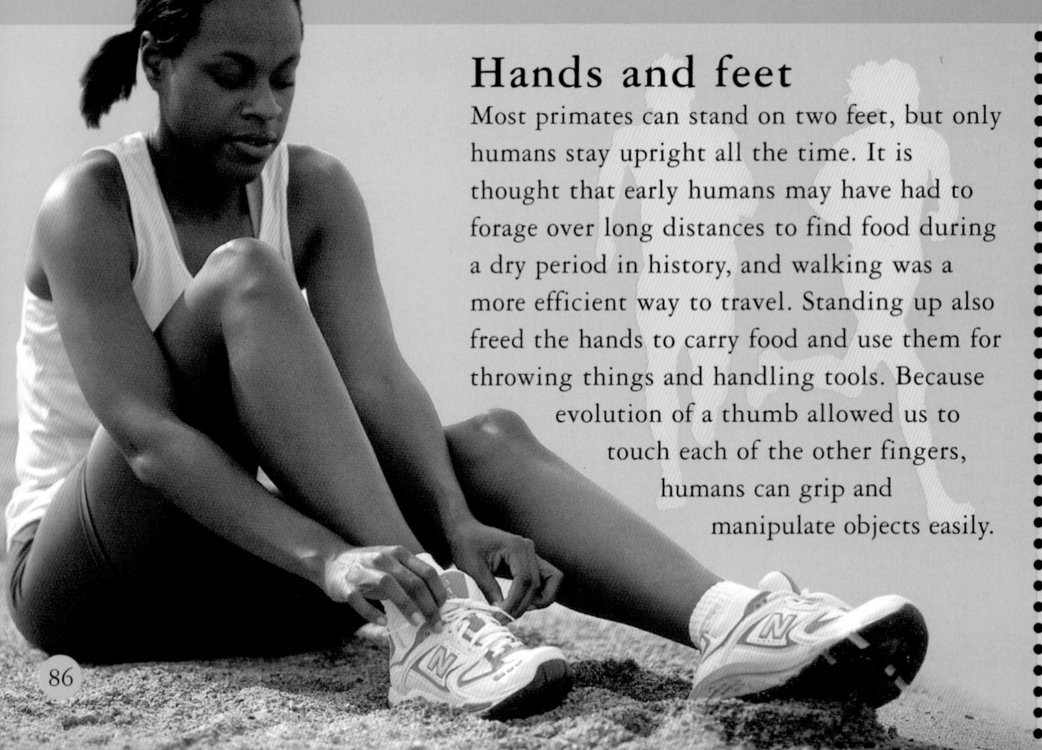

Hands and feet

Most primates can stand on two feet, but only humans stay upright all the time. It is thought that early humans may have had to forage over long distances to find food during a dry period in history, and walking was a more efficient way to travel. Standing up also freed the hands to carry food and use them for throwing things and handling tools. Because evolution of a thumb allowed us to touch each of the other fingers, humans can grip and manipulate objects easily.

Lack of hair

Humans have very little hair compared to other primates. It is thought we may have evolved this feature because:

1. it made it easier to forage for food in shallow water
2. it helped us lose heat faster on the hot savannas
3. it helped to reduce numbers of parasites on the body.

Luckily, humans learned to catch animals and used their skins to keep warm at night.

gradually changed the shape of the face and skull. It is thought that the australopithecines were the ancestors of the earliest species of *Homo*. This new branch of upright hominins developed an advantage by using tools and hunting for meat. Improvements in the diet led to increases in brain size and abilities. They developed language, began to live in communities, and worked together in groups. *Homo sapiens* emerged 250,000 years ago, and you are a descendant.

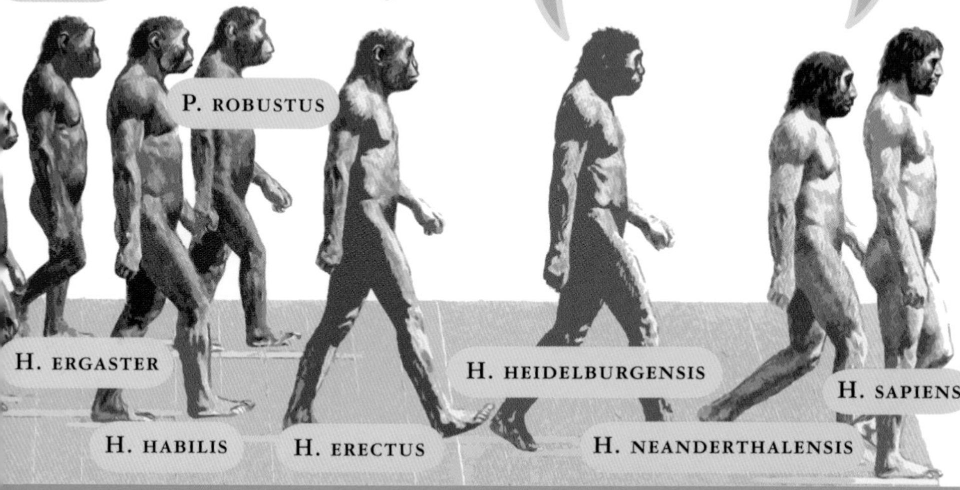
I'm very handy with stone tools—a real chip off the old flint.
With my posture I can walk tall in hunter-gatherer society.
Since I moved to Europe my hunting skills have improved enormously.
My brain's bigger than yours, even if you are better looking and less hairy than me.
P. BOISEI
P. ROBUSTUS
H. ERGASTER
H. HABILIS
H. ERECTUS
H. HEIDELBURGENSIS
H. NEANDERTHALENSIS
H. SAPIENS

Relative facts

Hobbits

The discovery of very small hominin fossils has led to debate about whether this is a new species, *Homo floresiensis,* or a human population that suffered from dwarfism. If it is a new species then it is the longest lasting non-modern human, having died out only about 12,000 years ago.

Your inner fish

The fact that humans hiccup may date back to our watery ancestors. Wiring in the brain that pushes water over fish gills and makes amphibians gulp air has been imperfectly rewired in mammals. It can make the diaphragm go into spasms, causing hiccups.

species went before us, but we are the only one left.

Increasing brain size

One of the most significant human evolution trends was the increase in brain size from 24 in³ (400 cm³) to around 85 in³ (1,400 cm³) today. Scientists think that as our diet improved, including more protein, fat, and better carbohydrates, this provided more energy for brain function so the brain could grow, which in turn led to greater intelligence and skills.

It's the wrinkly parts of my brain that give me my social skills, working memory, language, and sensory abilities.

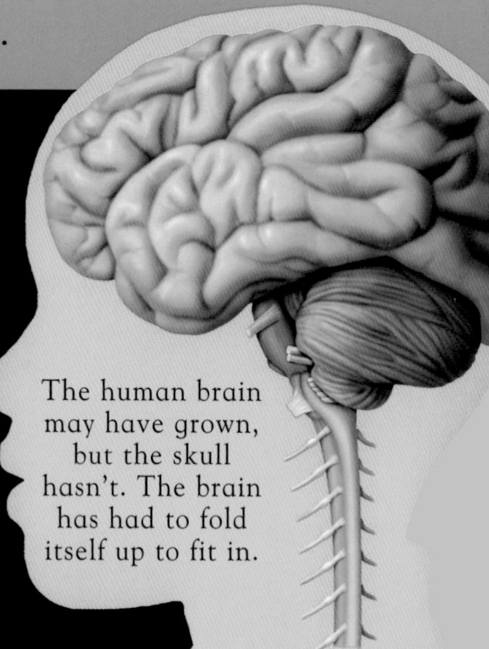

The human brain may have grown, but the skull hasn't. The brain has had to fold itself up to fit in.

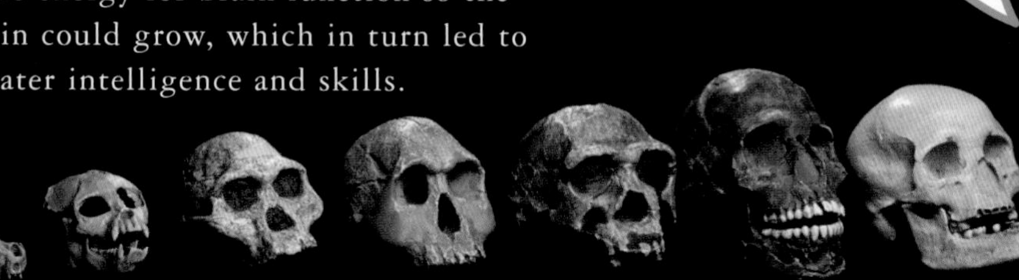

Brain size gradually increased as we progressed from an ape to a modern human.

HUMAN *behavior*

Why do we behave the way we do? While it's obvious that our bodies have evolved physically, our minds have also made great evolutionary leaps. However, there are still many things we do instinctively that have their origins in the past.

Start here

One of the main differences between humans and other animals is language. Our ability to communicate began with simple hand gestures and sounds that represented specific things. Gradually, we began to combine these to express ideas that were impossible with single words. As patterns developed in how words were used, they became the rules of grammar. This allows us to express any number of ideas with a limited set of words.

FACIAL EXPRESSIONS

We make faces every day, often without realizing we're doing it. They convey distinct meanings without the need for words. Some evolved as a way to express feelings and change other people's reactions to us. Others, like disgust, are a physical reaction to a particular stimulus

HAPPINESS

SADNESS

ANGER

FEAR

Many facial expressions

Hunters vs. Gatherers

Many male and female behaviors date back to our hunter-gatherer ancestors, where men brought home the mammoth steaks and women looked after the cave and the kids. This is probably why men can read maps and women like shopping—it's all down to our days on the savanna.

Hunters had to remember points in the landscape (hence map-reading skills).

Gatherers searched for the best fruit bushes (a little like shopping).

Aggression came from defending territory, confronting wild animals, and waging war.

Caring instinct developed from bringing up young and looking after the rest of the tribe.

Better at running, jumping, throwing, and catching mammoths.

Better at handling small objects and remembering where things are.

Like to compete against each other, and in teams against rival tribes.

Prefer to get along with everybody for tribal harmony and cooperation.

View relationships with others in terms of hierarchy (who is top dog).

View relationships in terms of family, emotional, and social bonds.

Communicate as a means to solve problems and to establish rank.

Communicate to establish social connections and intimacy.

Prefer to play games that have fixed rules, are competitive, and end with winners and losers.

Prefer to play games where all players do the same thing, such as skating or riding.

Baby talk

All babies have an inborn ability to learn language. They pick up words simply by listening to people around them. As they get older, the patterns of a language get fixed into their brains. Adults often find it hard to learn new languages because it is difficult to fix new patterns of grammar in an already "hard-wired" brain.

DISGUST

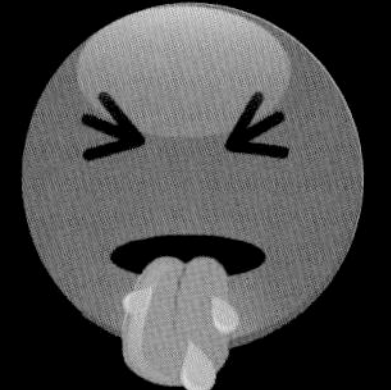

SURPRISE

INTEREST

are universal.

Humor

All humans instinctively laugh, but how do we recognize a joke? One possibility is that our brain recognizes a pattern and is surprised by it. Babies laugh at games that involve surprises, such as peekaboo, before they learn to talk. As we get older we start recognizing patterns in language. Jokes are just surprising uses of language we respond to by laughing.

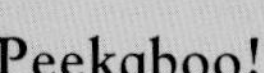

Surviving sickness

For all our brain power, physical ability, and sheer ingenuity, the human body is far from perfect. It can be attacked by invading organisms, has parts we don't need, and mechanisms that work too well. So why, despite all our other evolutionary advances, are we still so vulnerable to disease?

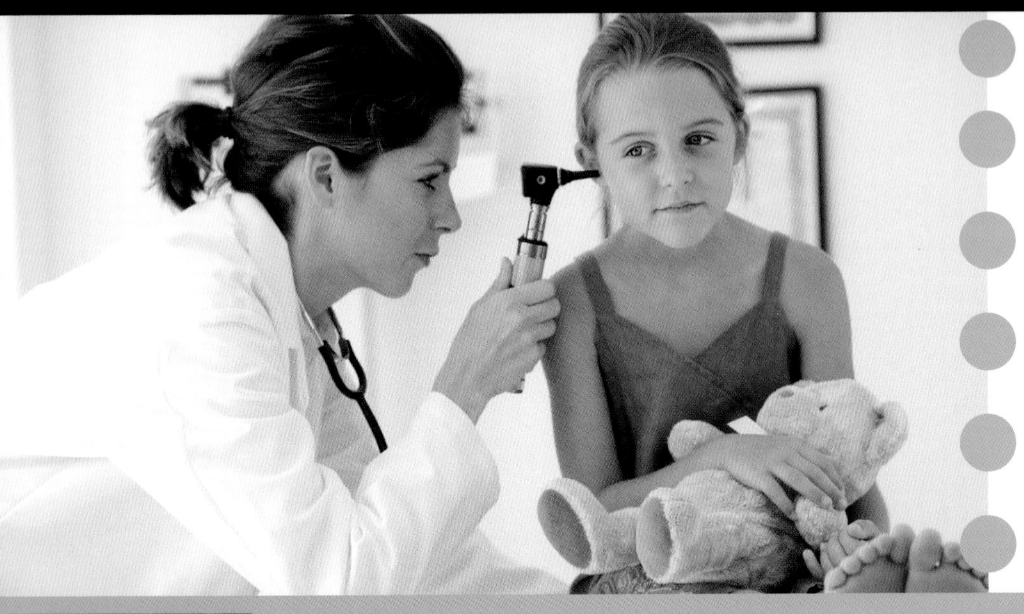

Back to nature

All living things get sick, and humans are no different. Many doctors are now looking at how evolution has shaped the human body and its systems and why it has left us with so many problems. Illnesses can be caused by faulty genes, invading bugs, design defects, and our own defense mechanisms. We are also facing new problems that nature hasn't had time to deal with. Examining our past may help us to have a healthier future.

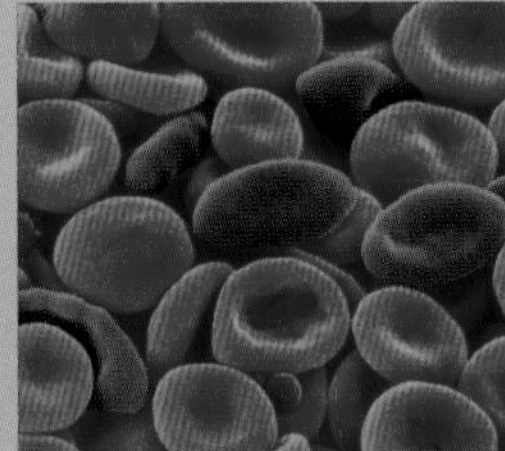

Upsides and downsides

Sickle-cell anemia is a common disease. It affects red blood cells, bending them into a rigid shape that makes them get stuck in blood vessels. People who inherit a copy of the sickle-cell gene from each parent suffer painful attacks and tend to die young. However, people who have one or both of the genes are resistant to malaria, which kills many people in hot countries. People without sickle cell genes are more likely to get malaria, so even though it causes disease, sickle cell has benefits and that is why the gene survives.

Defense mechanisms

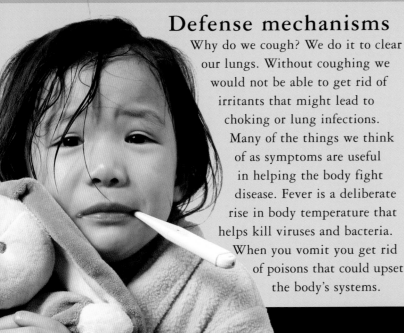

Why do we cough? We do it to clear our lungs. Without coughing we would not be able to get rid of irritants that might lead to choking or lung infections. Many of the things we think of as symptoms are useful in helping the body fight disease. Fever is a deliberate rise in body temperature that helps kill viruses and bacteria. When you vomit you get rid of poisons that could upset the body's systems.

Leftovers

The appendix is a little piece of intestine that seems to have no useful purpose. In theory, evolution should have gotten rid of it ages ago, because if it becomes infected it can kill us. Doctors now think it may be a place where gut bacteria hide during a bout of diarrhea. Its size seems to be crucial. A small, thin appendix is more likely to become inflamed, so selection may be favoring large appendixes.

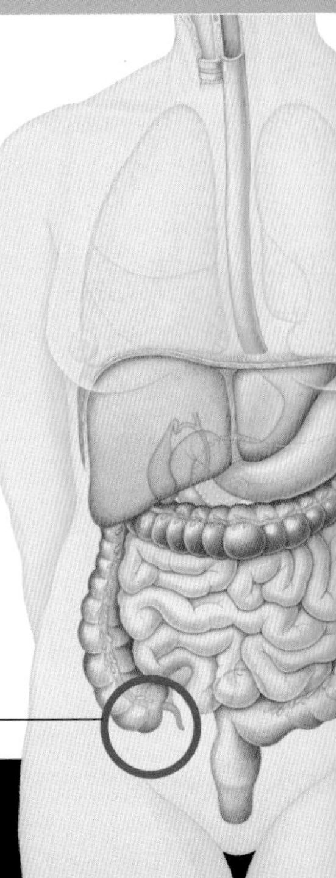

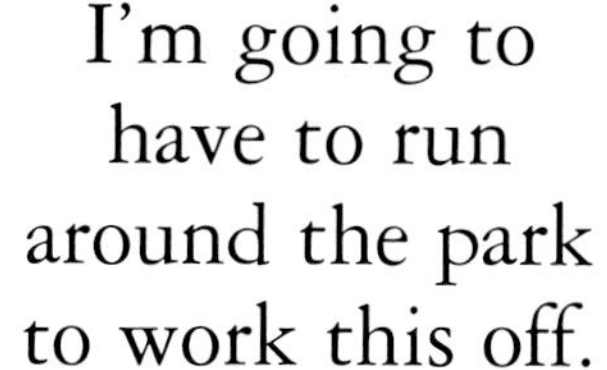

I'm going to
have to run
around the park
to work this off.

Too much fat

Back when man was a hunter-gatherer, foods containing fat and sugar were rare in the diet. People who could eat large amounts of these foods and put on weight quickly had an advantage in surviving famines. Today these foods are plentiful, but we still have the urge to eat as much of them as possible. Humans now face problems with obesity, diabetes, and heart disease because we don't do enough exercise to burn up the excess fat and sugar.

Beating the bugs

Many diseases in humans are caused by bacteria. Natural selection favors the bacteria because they can reproduce every 15 minutes and evolve to a new strain in as little as a day. Antibiotics have helped us fight infections but have also helped the bacteria by killing off weaker strains. This has left us with drug-resistant varieties that are extremely difficult to control.

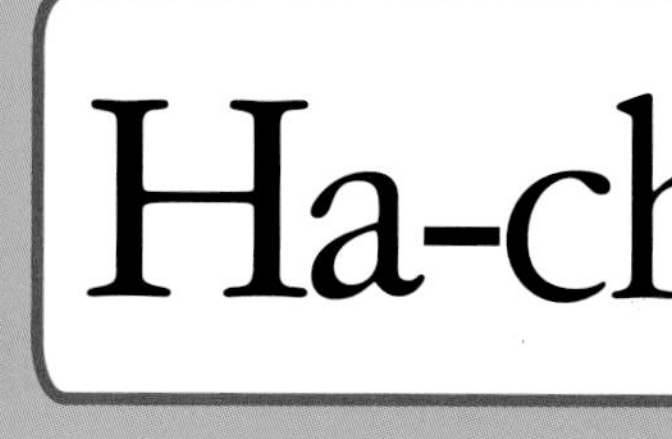

Ha-choo!

Our immune system is a mechanism that has evolved to combat **invading organisms.** It produces molecules called antibodies that stick to an invader so that IT CAN BE ENGULFED by a white blood cell. Sometimes the system goes into ***overdrive,*** producing an extreme allergic reaction to harmless things such as POLLEN or peanuts. This can be ***highly dangerous.*** Scientists hope to design a drug that can prevent these reactions from becoming **fatal.**

Sneezing is an allergic response. It can blast irritants out of the body at 100 mph (160 kph).

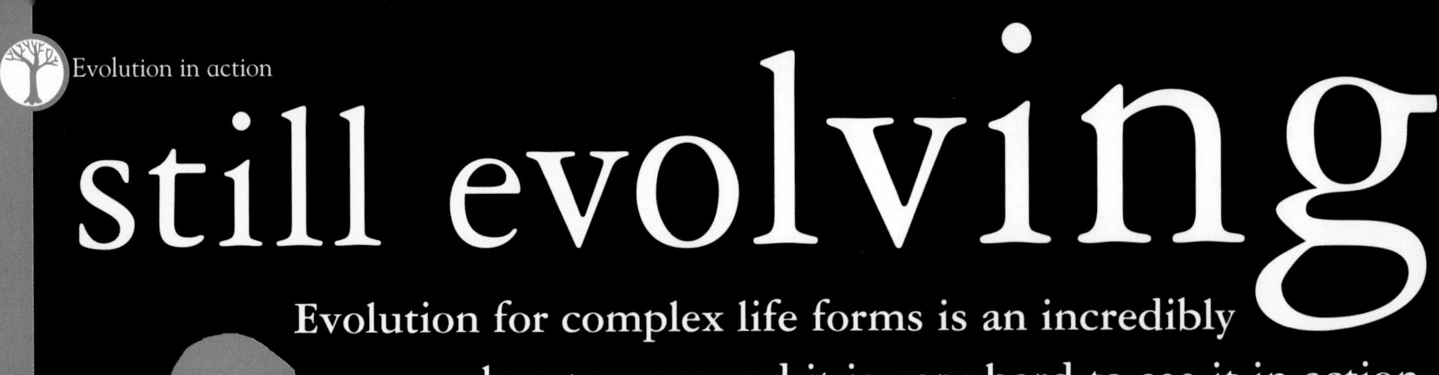

still evolving

Evolution for complex life forms is an incredibly slow process and it is very hard to see it in action.

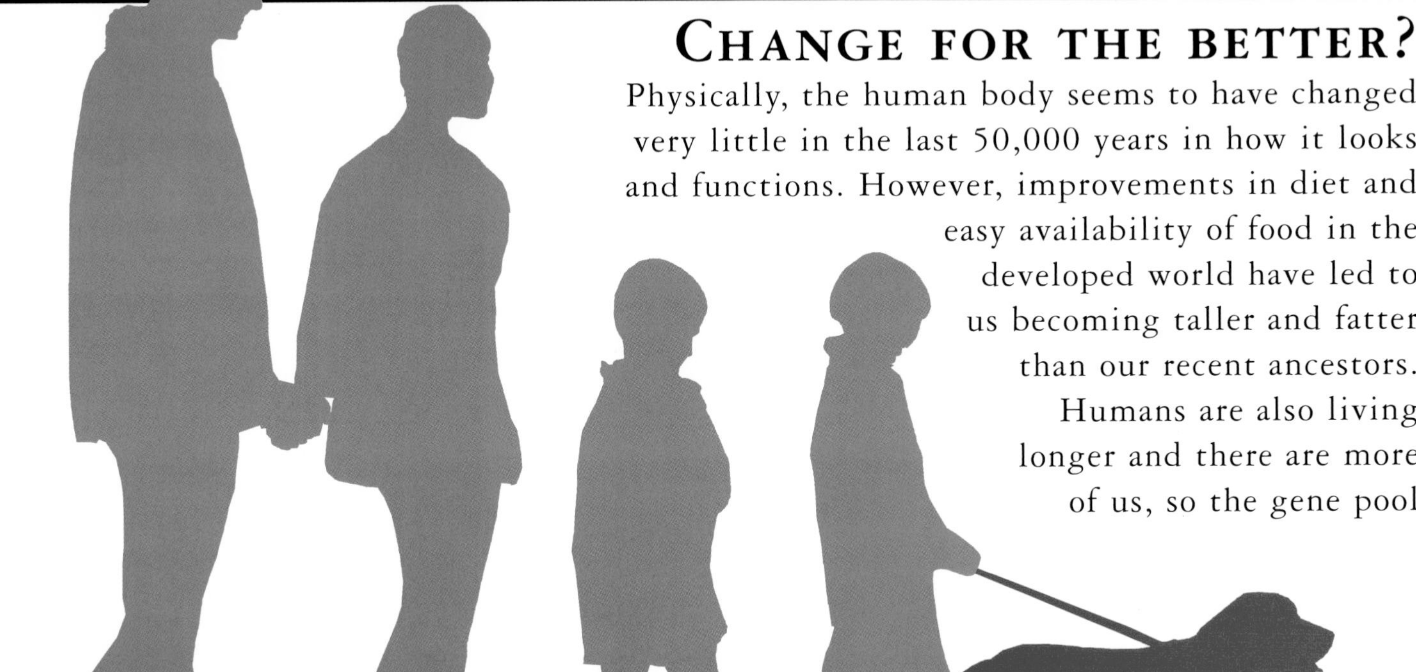

Change for the better?

Physically, the human body seems to have changed very little in the last 50,000 years in how it looks and functions. However, improvements in diet and easy availability of food in the developed world have led to us becoming taller and fatter than our recent ancestors. Humans are also living longer and there are more of us, so the gene pool

It may take thousands of ***generations*** before every

Genetic selection

I'd like a girl with blue eyes and brown hair, please.

New technology may have a more rapid effect on human evolution by allowing humans to choose what features their children are born with, such as intelligence or hair color. This could create ethical problems over whether we should try to eliminate "undesirable" traits, such as aggression or hereditary disease, or keep them in the gene pool.

Special powers

We don't have any superheroes who can fly or see through brick walls without mechanical help, but could it happen one day? It would take a lot of changes in our genes before humans could fly. It is impossible to reintroduce a trait once the genes have been lost, and our last ancestor with wing potential went on to become a bat rather than Batman.

Genetic changes are highly unpredictable and happen in response to changes in our environment. Scientists are divided about whether humans are still evolving or if we have reached our biological peak. Who knows where we might go from here?

is acquiring mutations faster than ever. But now that we have more control over our environment other things may start to drive evolutionary change. We can now use biotechnology to change our genes, so our future may be in our own hands.

member of a **population** shows a favorable *adaptation*.

The ultimate upload

One possible route science may take us along is a merger of man and technology. We already use bionics to replace defective limbs and organs. It may one day be possible to implant chips in the brain that make up for loss of speech or vision, or allow us to do things we're not good at. Imagine uploading a new learning program instead of doing homework!

Yeah man, this low gravity is stretching me to the limit.

Life on other planets

Another way humans might take a new evolutionary path is if we colonize other planets. Colonizers would face new environmental conditions, such as low gravity or lack of oxygen, that require new adaptations. Over centuries the colonizers (and any animals and plants that they took with them) would evolve to look, think, and behave differently.

GLOSSARY

Adaptation an inherited feature of a living thing that helps it to survive and reproduce in its environment.

Amphibian an animal, such as a frog or newt. Most need water in which to lay their eggs.

Ancestor an individual who lived in the past from whom other individuals have descended.

Arthropods invertebrate animals with a hard external skeleton and paired jointed legs. They include insects and crustaceans.

Artificial selection the process of selectively breeding plants and animals over time.

Australopithecine an early form of human that lived in Africa.

Bacteria microscopic single-celled organisms, some of which cause disease.

Biodiversity the number and variety of species living in a specific area or region.

Biotechnology the science of altering an organism's genes.

Botanist a person who studies plants.

Carnivore an animal that eats mainly meat.

Cell one of the microscopic structures that make up living things. Cells normally have an outer membrane, a jellylike filling, and a nucleus in the middle.

Characteristics the many variations of a gene.

Chromosome a threadlike structure in a cell's nucleus that contains DNA.

Classification the organization of different living things into related groups.

Common ancestor the most recent species from which two different species evolved.

Convergent evolution the process where organisms that are not related independently evolve similar traits as a result of having to adapt to a similar environment.

Crinoid an ancient group of invertebrates that includes sea lilies and feather stars that still exists today.

Cycad a palm-treelike plant.

DNA deoxyribonucleic acid, a very long double helix-shaped molecule (group of atoms) that carries genetic information as a chemical code.

Diversification a process of increasing variation among organisms that may lead to the development of new species.

Dominant gene a gene that has priority over a recessive (weaker) gene.

Embryo an organism in its early stages of development.

Evolution the process of change over time that occurs due to natural selection.

Extinction the disappearance of a species or a population.

Fertilization the fusion of male and female sex cells to create an embryo.

Fossils remains or traces of long-dead plants and animals that have been preserved in rock.

Gene a section of inherited code in DNA, which, when switched on, causes a specific reaction in a cell.

Gene flow the spread of genes from one population to another by migration and interbreeding.

Gene pool the total of all the genetic variations of a population.

Generation a group of individuals born and living at the same time.

Genetic bottleneck loss of genetic variations caused by a dramatic reduction in a species' population.

Genetic drift random changes in the frequency of traits in a population that occur by chance; one of the processes that drives evolution.

Genetics the study of genes and their effects.

Genetic variation the variety of genes present in a population through inheritance of genetic material.

Genome all the genetic information of a living thing.

Geologist a person who studies the origin and structure of Earth and its rock formations.

Habitat the area or environment in which an organism lives.

Hominin name for the evolutionary line, including the australopithecines, that led to modern humans, after they split off from chimpanzees and apes.

Hunter-gatherer description of how our early ancestors lived by hunting for animals and gathering fruit, seeds, and other plant material for eating.

Hybrid offspring produced by the breeding between individuals from different species.

Immune system the body's defense against invading organisms and foreign substances.

Invertebrate an animal that does not have a backbone.

Marsupial a group of mammals that give birth to underdeveloped young, which they then carry in a pouch. Kangaroos and koalas are marsupials.

Mollusk an invertebrate animal that has a soft body and often a hard outer shell. Snails and clams are mollusks.

Mutation a sudden change to a gene that results in genetic variation if inherited. The change can have either no effect, a harmful effect, or a helpful effect.

Natural selection the theory proposed by Darwin that is one of the processes causing evolution; individuals with the most favorable characteristics are more likely to survive.

Naturalist a person who studies plants and animals.

Neanderthal a recent hominin that lived at the same time as modern man, but who disappeared 25,000 years ago.

New World the continent of North and South America.

Niche the space and role occupied by an organism in an environment.

Nocturnal describes an animal that is active at night.

Nucleic acid a long, complex organic molecule such as DNA.

Old World the continents of Europe, Asia, and Africa.

Organism a living thing.

Ozone a toxic type of oxygen molecule that forms a layer in the atmosphere and prevents harmful radiation from reaching Earth.

Pangaea a supercontinent of all Earth's landmasses that formed in the late Permian and began to split apart in the Jurassic.

Parallel evolution where two related species evolve similar traits at the same time even though they are geographically separated.

Period a division of geological time. Each is given a name, such as Cambrian, Silurian, Triassic, Jurassic, and so on.

Pollination the transfer of pollen from the male part to the female part of a flower.

Population a group of individuals of the same species.

Predator an animal that hunts and feeds on another.

Primates the group of mammals that includes apes and humans.

Primitive describes an early undeveloped characteristic seen in an ancestor.

Pterosaur an extinct flying reptile with featherless membrane wings.

Recessive gene a gene that is only expressed in the absence of a dominant gene.

Reproduction the production of offspring during which genes are passed on from the parent or parents.

Reptile an animal that crawls on its belly or walks on short legs and whose skin is covered in bony plates or scales. Lizards are reptiles.

Sauropod a four-legged, plant-eating dinosaur that had a small head and a long neck and tail. Brachiosaurs were sauropods.

Savanna a tropical grassland with drought-resistant plants (mainly grasses) and few trees.

Sexual selection a form of natural selection where an individual selects a mate with a preferred characteristic.

Speciation the formation of a new species.

Species a group of related organisms that are capable of interbreeding to produce fertile offspring.

Subspecies a local population of a species that has slight genetic differences to the parent species but can still interbreed with it.

Tetrapod a land-walking vertebrate animal that has four limbs.

Trait a feature determined by a gene or a group of genes.

Trilobite a type of ancient marine arthropod.

Variation a difference in the structural or functional characteristics of an organism that is not seen in the rest of the species or population.

Vertebrate an animal that has a backbone.

Zoologist a person who studies animals and their behavior.

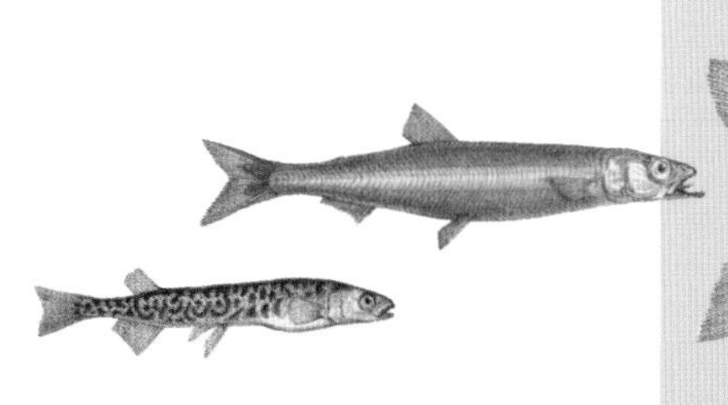

INDEX

adaptation 17, 23, 34, 51, 54, 93
appendix 90
artificial selection 17, 28, 29
Australia 74–75
bacteria 66, 81, 90, 91
Beagle, HMS 15, 22–23
bees 58–59
Bible 11, 12, 14
biodiversity 60
biotechnology 61, 92, 93
birds 26, 59, 62–63, 70, 72, 77
brain 87
Buffon, Comte de 12
Cambrian period 67, 68
camouflage 32, 48
Carboniferous period 69
catastrophe theory 15
cats 48, 49, 71
cells 42–44, 66
chromosomes 42–44, 46, 47, 49
classification 12
cloning 61
common ancestor 12, 17, 25, 45, 80–81
competitive advantage 17, 32, 33, 34, 48
Covington, Syms 23
Creation 10–11, 35
Cretaceous period 70
cross-pollination 29, 32, 33
Cuvier, Georges 14, 15
Darwin, Charles 6–7, 16–39, 43, 54, 73, 86
Darwin, Erasmus 20
Devonian period 69
dinosaurs 62–63, 70, 71
diseases 56, 90–91
DNA 44–45, 49, 57, 62, 63, 66
dogs 17, 43, 78
ears 73
Earth 11, 14, 66
elephants 84–85
embryos 78–79
environment 13, 56, 93
evolution 16–17, 28, 30–35, 45, 77
extinction 14, 53, 60, 70, 71
eyes 34–35, 47, 79
facial expressions 88
family trees 82–83
finches 23, 54–55
FitzRoy, Robert 22
flowers 26, 27, 32, 71, 72, 79
fossils 14–15, 27, 62, 65, 67, 72
frogs 30, 31, 72, 77
Galápagos Islands 23, 39, 54, 55, 74, 75
gene pool 52–53, 60
gene technology 60–61
genes 41–63, 93
genetic drift 52–53
genetic selection 92
genome 44–45
geological time 68–71
geology 15, 72
GM crops 61
gods 10, 11, 13
grandparents 56–57
Grant, Dr. Robert 21
Haeckel, Ernst 79
hair 51, 86
Henslow, J. 21, 22, 24
hiccups 87
Hooker, Joseph 25, 36
horses 78, 82–83
humans 12, 30
  behavior 88–89
  evolution 17, 65, 71, 78, 80, 86–87, 92–93
  genetics 42, 45, 47
humor 89
Huxley, Thomas 16
hybrids 29, 55
immune system 91
inheritance 13, 17, 43, 44, 46–49
insects 27, 33, 69, 70
  colonies 58–59
islands 74–75
Jurassic period 70
koalas 77
Lamarck, Chevalier de 13, 16, 57
language 88–89
lichens 67
life 66–71
Linnaeus, Carl 12
Lyell, Charles 15, 25, 36
Madagascar 74, 75
Malthus, Thomas 30
mammals 70, 71, 72
mammoths 62, 71, 85
Mendel, Gregor 42, 43
missing links 72–73
mutations 48–51, 52, 53, 60, 93
natural selection 16–17, 30–37, 41, 52, 53
Noah's flood 14, 15
Ordovician period 68
Paley, William 35
Pasteur, Louis 13
peacock 32
penguins 48, 49
Permian period 69
planet colonies 93
plants 26, 28, 29, 42, 43, 68–70
platypus 73
pollination 26, 27, 29, 70
quagga 83
Quaternary period 71
red kites 52–53
reptiles 69, 70
salamanders 72
seeds 28, 29, 30, 33, 72, 79
selective breeding 17, 28–29, 83
separation 54
sex chromosomes 47
Silurian period 68
speciation 54–55
species 6, 17, 12, 25
Spencer, Herbert 39
spots 79
stripes 48, 79
stromatolites 66
sundews 33
survival 31–33
Tennyson, Lord 30
Tertiary period 71
tetrapods 69, 72
Triassic period 70
twins 46, 50
Ussher, James 11
variation 16–17, 46, 48
Wallace, Alfred 36
wings 25, 76, 79, 92

Acknowledgments

Dorling Kindersley would like to thank Penny Smith for editorial help with this book and Peter Bull for the illustrations on pages 72 and 73.

The publisher would like to thank the following for their kind permission to reproduce their photographs:

(Key: a-above; b-below/bottom; c-center; f-far; l-left; r-right; t-top)

akg-images: Erich Lessing 10cra; **Alamy Images:** APIX 30b; Arco Images / W. Dolder 81bl (hyrax); Erwan Balanca / Jupiterimages / Stock Image 31tr; David Ball 24cb; Peter Barritt 52cra; birdpix 52c; blickwinkel 49bl; Brandon Cole Marine Photography 35br; Nigel Cattlin 58-59; David Chapman 53cr; FLPA 53fbl; Chris Fredriksson 48cr; Bob Gibbons 29bc; Nick Greaves 77cla; Tim Hill 28tr; David Hosking 48c; Interfoto Pressebildagentur 12cla; Janine Wiedel Photolibrary 40bl; Piotr & Irena Kolasa 79clb; Dennis Kunkel / Phototake Inc. 90cl; Lebrecht Music and Arts Photo Library 5cla, 21cb, 24cla; The London Art Archive 13cr, 19clb, 25crb, 36crb; Celia Mannings 74br; Mary Evans Picture Library 11b, 15tl, 17bl, 20bc, 30tr, 38 (Emma Darwin), 38cra, 42clb, 43tr; moodboard 60tr; Keith Morris 91br; Tsuneo Nakamura / Volvox Inc. 34-35b (water); Natural History Museum, London 36clb; The Natural History Museum 24tl, 83br; Nature Alan King 67cla; North Wind Picture Archives 23tc, 38c (Darwin); Old Paper Studios 38-39t (piano); Ian Paterson 10cla; Paul Thompson Images 53cra; Miguel Angel Muñoz Pellicer 12cra; Photodisc 67b; Phototake Inc. 66c; The Print Collector 15cr, 20br, 27cr, 30cra (Malthus), 72bl; Robert Harding Picture Library Ltd. 54cr; David J. Slater 53br; David Tipling 32cr; Jeff Tucker 27cl; Rob Walls 18cl; Dave Watts 73cra; WorldFoto 77cra; **Ardea:** Chris Harvey 59tr; Steve Hopkin 58ca, 58cb; **The Art Archive:** Gemaldegalerie, Dresden 11t; **Auckland Museum:** 25cl; **British Library:** 85tl; **Corbis:** Heide Benser / zefa 47br (freckles); K. & H. Benser / zefa 74bl, 75clb, 75crb (rafts); Tom Brakefield 76ca; Tim Davis / Davis Lynn Wildlife 11cl; Nigel J. Dennis / Gallo Images 76cra; DLILLC / Davis Lynn Wildlife 48br; Historical Picture Archive 17ca; Images.com 92br; Peter Johnson 75ca (tenrec); Frans Lanting 2fcrb, 3clb (*Psilotum nudum*), 65bl, 68cr; Joe McDonald 76cla; moodboard 61crb; Arthur Morris 77clb; Jim Richardson 61tr; Galen Rowell 75br; Staffan Widstrand 77ca; **Reproduced with permission from John van Wyhe ed., The Complete Work of Charles Darwin Online (http://darwin-online.org.uk/):** 6 (sidebar), 6bc, 6br, 6ftr, 6t (frogs), 6tl, 6tl (fish), 6-7bc, 7 (sidebar), 7bc, 7br, 7ftl, 7ftr, 7tl, 7tr, 15br, 16bl (book, 16tl, 17bc (chimp), 17bc (expressions), 17br, 18bc, 18tl, 19 (moths), 19tl, 20, 22b (chart), 22ca (Beagle), 22-23bc, 23br, 23cl, 23tl, 23tr, 25cr, 30-31 (b/w frogs), 37cr (insert), 37crb, 54cl, 72-73 (diagram background), 94br, 94cl, 94crb, 94fcra, 94tr, 95bl, 95br, 95cra, 95fbl, 95tl; **DK Images:** Booth Museum of Natural History, Brighton 74fcl (platypus); Philip Dowell 79tr; Hunterian Museum and Art Gallery, University of Glasgow 69ca; London Butterfly House, Syon Park 21t (butterflies), 95cb; Sonia Moore 27b (boxes); Natural History Museum, London 3clb, 5tl, 14cb, 15clb, 25bl, 33cb (bumble bee), 71bc, 78clb, 84cla, 84clb, 84cra, 84crb, 85cla, 96tl; Oxford University Museum of Natural History 31tl; Rough Guides 10l (vegetation); Royal Geographical Society, London 18tr; The Science Museum, London 19cla, 21l (flask), 96tc; The Home of Charles Darwin, Down House (English Heritage) 26tl; The Home of Charles Darwin, Down House (English Heritage) / Natural History Museum, London 22clb; Barrie Watts 53bl; Jerry Young 74fclb (echidna); **Reprinted with permission from Encyclopædia Britannica, © 2005 by Encyclopædia Britannica, Inc.:** 55 (finches); **The English Heritage Photo Library:** 18c, 26cl; By kind permission of Darwin Heirlooms Trust 20tr; **Getty Images:** American Images Inc. 47c (dimples); Torbjorn Arvidson / Nordic Photos 60b; The Bridgeman Art Library 8-9, 9bl (monkey), 14-15b, 22cl, 22tr, 22-23c (sea), 33tl; Alice Edward / Stone 34tl (jar); Jamie Grill / Iconica 90cla; Hulton Archive 20crb; Jeff Hunter / Photographer's Choice 60ca; John Lamb / Stone 61tl; Régine Mahaux / Riser 10br (man); Mark Moffett / Minden Pictures 54br; Jeff Sherman 93bl; Scott Sroka / National Geographic 63br; ZSSD / Minden Pictures 50cb; **Matthew Harris / John F. Fallon at the University of Wisconsin-Madison:** 62bl; **iStockphoto.com:** Roman Kobzarev 32c; Alexandre Zveiger 47bl (hand); **Courtesy Thomas J. Lemieux:** 73tl; **Mary Evans Picture Library:** 16b (Huxley), 16b (Wilberforce), 16cr, 21bl, 21c; **Sean McCann:** 79bc; **National Library Of Scotland:** Reproduced with permission of the Trustees of the National Library of Scotland 16cl; **The Natural History Museum, London:** 23bc, 26bl, 26crb, 26tr, 27cla, 27cra, 67tc; **PA Photos:** Barry Batchelor / PA Archive 51bl; **Dr Andrew Pask:** 63ca; **Photolibrary:** Nicholas Eveleigh / Digital Vision 26-27c, 84-85b; Nick Koudis / Photodisc 47fbr; Oxford Scientific (OSF) / Carlos Sanchez Alonso 53cl; Photodisc 37; PureStock 77fcra; Stockbyte 91tl; **Photoshot:** Mark Fairhurst / UPPA 27fcl; **Science Photo Library:** 15cra, 51tl; Michael Abbey 67cl; Mauricio Anton 87tr; Sally Bensusen 69br; Annabella Bluesky 47cl; Tony Camacho 50bl; Michael Clutson 49cb; Ted Clutter 70cl; CNRI 49ca; Lynette Cook 66ftl, 67cr; Darwin Dale 58crb; Christian Darkin 70bl, 83bc, 83c; Dept. Of Clinical Cytogenetics, Addenbrookes Hospital 47cl, 47crb, 47fclb, 47fcrb; Georgette Douwma 34bl, 66cr; Pascal Goetgheluck 86tl, 87bl (skulls); Patrick Lynch 34fbl; Dr. P. Marazzi 50br; Tom Mchugh 34br; Mark Miller 87crb (brain); Dr. G. Moscoso 64tl; Pasieka 44crb; Raul Gonzalez Perez 34tl, 34tl (eye balls); Philippe Plailly / Eurelios 3bc (modern man), 71fcrb; Philippe Psaila 45clb; Nemo Ramjet 3br, 93bc; James H. Robinson 50c; P. Rona / OAR / National Undersea Research Program / NOAA 66tl; Kaj R. Svensson 68c; Joe Tucciarone 2tl, 70cb; Lena Untidt / Bonnier Publications 58cra; L. Willatt, East Anglian Regional Genetics Service 43bc; **Shutterstock:** 36-37b; alle 59tl; Nick Biemans 45bc; Bryan Busovicki 39bc; Cheryl Casey 47fbl; Chiyacat 29ca; Paul Cowan 28cra; John de la Bastide 29b; Adem Demir 41tl; Miodrag Gajic 51crb; garloon 38cra (trumpet); János Gehring 72-73 (background); Gelpi 64cl; Angelo Gilardelli 41bl; GoodMood Photo 24r; Eric Isselée 5clb, 40tr; javarman 12cra (books); Adrian T. Jones 32cl; Sebastian Kaulitzki 40cl; Christopher King 36l; Oleg Kozlov, Sophy Kozlova 45crb; Kudryashka 76-77 (globes); Timur Kulgarin 18bl; Sergey Lavrentev 45cb; LiveStock 88-89b; Maugli 25; Najin 75t (paper); Andrei Nekrassov 34fbr; Donald P. Oehman 39clb; Kirsty Pargeter 40crb; Thomas M. Perkins 90bl; Florin Tirlea 24r (pile); Irina Tischenko 45br; Shachar Weis 29br; **Still Pictures:** BIOS, François Gilson 31br; **SuperStock:** Jaime Abecasis 9br; **University of Calgary:** Ken Bendiktsen / Jason Anderson 72crb; **University of Chicago. Model by Tyler Keillor, photo by Beth Rooney:** 72cr (Tiktaalik).

Jacket images: Front: **DK Images:** The National Birds of Prey Centre, Gloucestershire clb (eagle); Natural History Museum, London tl (*Phiomia*); Jerry Young bc (crocodile), fbl (leopard); **Getty Images:** Zubin Shroff / Stone+ b (background); **PunchStock:** Digital Vision / Y. Taro c. Back: **Reproduced with permission from John van Wyhe ed., The Complete Work of Charles Darwin Online (http://darwin-online.org.uk/):** cla, tl; **Science Photo Library:** Kaj R. Svensson br.